D0805112

GORDON

MILITARY PROFILES

SERIES EDITOR

Dennis E. Showalter, Ph.D.
Colorado College

Instructive summaries for general and expert
readers alike, volumes in the Military Profiles
series are essential treatments of significant and
popular military figures drawn from world history,
ancient times through the present.

GORDON

Victorian Hero

C. Brad Faught

Potomac Books, Inc.
Washington, D.C.

Copyright © 2008 Potomac Books, Inc.

Published in the United States by Potomac Books, Inc. All rights reserved.
No part of this book may be reproduced in any manner whatsoever without
written permission from the publisher, except in the case of brief quotations
embodied in critical articles and reviews.

Library of Congress Cataloging-in-Publication Data

Faught, C. Brad.
  Gordon : Victorian hero / C. Brad Faught.
     p. cm. — (Military profiles)
  Includes bibliographical references and index.
   ISBN-13: 978-1-59797-144-7 (hardcover : acid-free paper)
   ISBN-13: 978-1-59797-145-4 (pbk. : acid-free paper)
  1. Gordon, Charles George, 1833-1885. 2. Generals—Great
Britain—Biography. 3. Great Britain. Army—Biography. 4.
Sudan—History—1821-1881. I. Title.
  DA68.32.G6F37 2008
  962.4'03092—dc22

                              2007046146

(alk. paper)

Printed in the United States of America on acid-free paper that meets
the American National Standards Institute Z39-48 Standard.

Potomac Books, Inc.
22841 Quicksilver Drive
Dulles, Virginia 20166

First Edition

10 9 8 7 6 5 4 3 2 1

*To my wife, Rhonda,
my daughter, Claire,
and my son, Luke*

Contents

Every empire generates its own heroes. And in the British Empire in its late-Victorian heyday none achieved greater acclaim than Gen. Charles Gordon. During 1884 and early 1885, it is unlikely that anyone in the English-speaking world was more famous than Gordon, whose stout defense of the town and garrison of Khartoum in Sudan against its Islamic attackers proved enormously compelling. The Victorian public, by the 1880s highly literate and voracious readers of the popular press, and becoming increasingly used to heroic portrayals of imperial worthies in the newspapers, found in the saga of Gordon a story for the ages. Trapped in the middle of a million square miles of unforgiving Sudanese desert, supplies and morale running low in the face of thousands of so-called "Dervishes," intent on Islamic *jihad*, Gordon held out for ten months before finally being put to the sword in January 1885, two days before his fifty-second birthday. In a world that is riven by Islamism, and where Sudan holds the terrible distinction of being home to an ongoing genocide in its devastated province of Darfur, Gordon's story remains highly resonant.

Gordon's place in British imperial history was assured by the Sudan epic but not created by it. He had created his reputation during the previous thirty years, beginning with his commissioning in the Royal Engineers in 1852 and subsequent service in Crimea, China, Sudan—for the first time in the 1870s—and elsewhere. Indeed, as this book seeks to demonstrate, Gordon's experiences prior to Khartoum properly prepared him for the events in Sudan, and the fatalistic Gordon treated his predicament there as his final appointment with destiny.

There was no shortage of swordsmen in the British Empire. And as a military strategist or commander of armies, Gordon was not their equal.

However, Gordon was a skilled military engineer, an inspired leader of irregular troops, and utterly fearless in battle. His ability to convince non-European troops to fight in a European style was remarkable and the personal loyalty he engendered speaks to an interesting and not fully understood feature of the dynamic of imperial expansion. He demonstrated his character first in China, wading into the fray unarmed but for a stick that became known as his "wand of victory." Later, in Equatoria in southern Sudan, he temporarily broke up the Arab slave trade, perhaps the most brutal commerce found anywhere in late-nineteenth-century Africa, with a combination of lethal force and the persuasive power of his own personality.

That personality was the source of much speculation in Gordon's time and has been an inescapable part of any biographical treatment of him ever since. Previous biographers of Gordon have focused on what they considered his strange brand of Christian fundamentalism. This misplaced focus can be attributed to the writer Lytton Strachey. His book, *Eminent Victorians*, in which he wrote about "the end of General Gordon," planted a picture of a temperamental extremist, given to religious reverie and excessive, covert drinking in the public mind.[1] Despite the complete debunking of Strachey's misinformed polemic, this image of Gordon remains popular.[2]

Gordon was a deeply committed Christian. But his alleged religious fanaticism pales not only in comparison to what is seen in our own day, but even more clearly when compared to his last and greatest enemy, the Mahdi (the "Expected Guide," a messiah in Muslim tradition). Gordon was a mostly orthodox Christian sent by the Egyptian and British governments as their agent to undertake a military evacuation of Sudan. He made no efforts to convert Sudanese Muslims to Christianity. In contrast to Gordon, Mohammed Ahmed, known as the Mahdi in Sudan, was an Islamic extremist who believed that he was the Prophet's chosen successor and therefore would live to see the world bow before him. It is no coincidence that the Mahdi's grandson and former Sudanese prime minister, Sadiq al-Mahdi, helped pave the way for the current Sudanese Islamist regime of Omar al-Bashir. Under Omar's welcoming eye, Osama bin Laden founded al Qaeda while living in Sudan from 1994–98, in preparation for the terrorist attacks in the United States on September 11, 2001.[3]

Gordon's Christian faith defined his character, but he was also a career soldier who quickly came to terms with the conflicts between his faith and war, and whose military training prepared him for battle. The siege of Khartoum on January 26, 1885, when the Mahdi's *ansar* (helpers) overran the city's defenses and killed Gordon along with thousands of others, is not the moment of greatest interest for historians of the period. Rather, Gordon's place in the military history of the British Empire was established cumulatively so that even though the saga of Khartoum ended in defeat, it seemed a natural culmination of Gordon's martial career. Clive had his Plassey, Roberts his Kandahar, Kitchener his Omdurman. All were victories. And Gordon had his great victory too: in China, at Soochow, in 1863. But in 1885 at Khartoum Gordon lost. The city fell, the garrison was wiped out, and his decapitated head was displayed on a pole planted in the Mahdi's camp. Still, more than a century later, a span of time that saw the collapse of the British Empire, Gordon remains a powerful military symbol of that great swath of territory upon which it was said the sun never set.

Despite the single name on the cover, the writing of a book is never a solitary endeavor. I would like to thank the staff of Potomac Books for their expert work, especially Katie Freeman, assistant editor, and Jen Waldrop, assistant production editor. Equally, I would like to thank the librarians, archivists, and staff of the British Library, Manuscripts Room; the National Archives, Kew; St. Antony's College, Oxford, Middle East Centre; the Royal Engineers Museum, Chatham; the National Portrait Gallery, London; the Bridgeman Art Library International, the University of Toronto, Robarts Library; and the Toronto Public Library. My thanks also to Gordon's School in Woking, England, and its Headmaster, Denis Mulkerrin; to Roy Newman, National Secretary of the Old Gordonian Association; and to Andrew Gregg, longtime friend and former colleague, for drawing the maps. Trevor Lloyd, Emeritus Professor of History at the University of Toronto and a distinguished scholar of the British Empire, kindly read the manuscript. His suggestions have made it a better book, for which I am grateful. My home institution, Tyndale University College in Toronto, granted me a sabbatical during which most of the research and writing of this book was completed. Tyndale also has been generous with research funds on this and other occasions. A word of thanks, as well, to Brad Longard, faculty research assistant at Tyndale, for compiling bibliographies.

While carrying out research in the United Kingdom, I enjoyed staying, reading, and writing at the Travellers Club in London. I would like to thank the staff of the Club, as well as my fellow members, for such a wonderful setting in which to think about all things Gordon. Additionally, during my sabbatical I had the pleasure of making Massey College in the University of Toronto my temporary academic home. My thanks to John Fraser, Master of the College, for appointing me a Senior Resident.

Finally, the dedication of this book speaks to the gratitude I have for my family. Their happy forbearance allows me to keep returning in my mind to the Victorian era from one that is most emphatically not.

Chronology

1833	born January 28 in Woolwich, England; grew up there and in Ireland, Corfu, and Scotland
1843–46	educated at Folland's House, a school near Taunton, Somerset
1846–47	attended Jeffries, a military crammer school in Shooter's Hill, Woolwich
1848	entered the Royal Military Academy at Woolwich
1852	commissioned as a second lieutenant in the Royal Engineers
1854	promoted to lieutenant and posted to Pembroke Dock, Wales
1855	arrived in Crimea
1856–58	surveyed the Danube and Armenia
1859–60	promoted to captain and posted to the Chatham depot
1860–64	in China, promoted to brevet major in 1862 and to lieutenant colonel in 1864
1865	posted to Gravesend as the officer in command
1871	named the British representative on the international Danube Commission
1872	promoted to brevet colonel
1873	appointed governor of Equatoria (southern Sudan)
1874	arrived in Khartoum
1877–79	appointed governor general of Sudan
1880	served as private secretary to Lord Ripon, viceroy of India, in China
1881	commanded the Royal Engineers in Mauritius
1882	promoted to major general; briefly posted in Cape Colony, South Africa

To the Army Born: Woolwich and Wales

Woolwich is an unprepossessing suburb of London known mainly for being the home of the Royal Military Academy (RMA), which specializes in training engineers and artillerymen for the British army. In 1833, four years before Victoria acceded to the throne and began the era that would come to bear her name, Woolwich stood outside the expanding reach of the great metropolis. It is appropriate that Charles George Gordon was born in Woolwich on January 28, 1833, because he became the most famous Royal Engineer, and for more than half a century a statue of him stood in London's Trafalgar Square, in the shadow only of the great Admiral Nelson's column.[1]

Gordon's military pedigree was long and distinguished. His was the fifth generation of his family to serve the crown. His father, Col. Henry William Gordon, an artillerymen, rose to the rank of lieutenant general. One of Charles's brothers, Enderby, also attained the rank of general, and another, Henry, was knighted. Altogether, Charlie (as he was called by family and friends) Gordon grew up in a family of eleven children presided over by the "firm yet genial" Colonel Gordon and his accommodating wife, Elizabeth Enderby.[2] The Enderbys had been successful ship owners, working primarily in the New England trade. They took tea to America and brought whale oil to England. Without an Enderby ship there would have been no Boston Tea Party in 1773. Later, however, the firm fell on hard times and went out of business.

The Gordons belonged to the Church of England. Elizabeth Enderby had a Unitarian background, but she too belonged to the established church owing to her father's move to social respectability earlier in the nineteenth century. For the young Charlie, church going was a rote affair, part of the normal ebb and flow of his upbringing; only later would his religiosity intensify and with it, his establishmentarianism weaken.

Gordon's earliest years were spent in a Woolwich terrace house. In 1836, the three-year-old Charlie began what would be a typical peripatetic military childhood. In that year, Colonel Gordon was posted to Dublin, in the last years before the devastating potato famine of the 1840s. In 1838 the family moved back across the Irish Sea to Leith Fort, located not far from Edinburgh. In 1840, the Colonel was ordered to Corfu in the Ionian Islands, a British holding leftover from the settlement of the Napoleonic Wars. Here the young Charlie would pass three delightful years in the bright sunshine and azure blue of the eastern Mediterranean, a stark contrast to the clouds and dampness of the British Isles.

Like most others of their class and station in Britain, the Gordon family employed both a nanny and a governess. Charlie's initial rudimentary education was under the province of the latter. He was a rambunctious child, given to pranks and occasional impudence. Earliest family recollections show him to have had a winning way nonetheless, a "robust playfulness of manner; and above all the twinkle of fun in his clear blue eyes."[3] His eyes, along with a tight, curly helmet of blond hair, were Gordon's greatest physical distinction. He was short, under the average for the time, and grew to be only 5'6". His frame was slight as a child, later becoming wiry and muscular with quick and economical movements to match.

Gordon's sunny Mediterranean reverie ended in 1843 when, as a ten-year-old, he was taken back to England to begin his formal education. The leading English public schools of the day, Eton, Harrow, Winchester, and others, had yet to undergo their "revolution" inspired by the headmaster of the Rugby School, Dr. Thomas Arnold.[4] Therefore, the Gordons shared the view of many of their peers that the great schools were vice ridden and corrupted their youthful charges. To some degree this view was a convenient caricature.[5] Nonetheless, it was a view held strongly and acted upon by the Gordons. Their governess, Miss Rogers, suggested instead that Charlie be sent to a small school run by her brother near the village of Taunton in Somerset. The school was new and had only twenty boarders, but the Reverend George Rogers was exactly the kind of steadying, religious influence deemed perfect for Charlie. In October 1843 he entered Folland's House, as the school was called.

For the next three years Gordon's waning childhood and early adolescence were passed under the benevolent tutelage of the Reverend Rogers. These otherwise placid years were spiked by two major events. The first was the early death of Gordon's favorite sister, his beloved Emily. Seven years his senior, she suffered from tuberculosis, known to Victorians as "consumption." Like so many of her peers in the nineteenth century, it killed her remorselessly. Emily Gordon was only seventeen when she died in November 1843. Young Charlie was devastated, remembering later that "humanly speaking it changed my life, it was never the same since."[6]

The other significant event in Charlie's life at this time was the return of the rest of the Gordon family to Woolwich from Corfu. In October 1845, Colonel Gordon undertook a new appointment at the Royal Artillery Barracks at Woolwich. Meanwhile at Folland's House, Charlie was proving to be a good, but in no way exceptional, student. To prepare for the Royal Military Academy's admission test, his parents decided that Charlie needed to attend an examination crammer. So from 1846–47 he attended Jeffries crammer school in Shooter's Hill, near Woolwich. When at home he continued to display the high spirits for which he had always been known. Colonel Gordon once remarked in reference to Charlie and his two other youngest sons, William and Freddie, that with them he was "sitting on a powder barrel."[7]

During this period Gordon grew closer to his sister, Augusta. She was eleven years older than him, but with Emily's passing she took on a much larger role in his young life, a position she would always maintain. Augusta never married and she became Charlie's confidante and refuge. Years later, it was from Augusta's white terrace house in Southampton, inherited from their parents, that Gordon would depart for London to discuss with, and then accept from Prime Minister William Gladstone's government his ultimate assignment in Khartoum.

Augusta's single biggest impact on Charlie was to ignite his latent religiosity. Augusta's influence over Charlie, sparked by Emily's death, became key in his religious life. She had had her own faith renewed by Capel Molyneux, the new curate at Holy Trinity, their Church of England parish in Woolwich. The persuasive preaching and high-minded example offered by Molyneux sealed Augusta's Christian devotion. She in turn attempted to impress on her family the necessity of spiritual commitment, and she had considerable success. The fourteen-year-old Charlie, however, did not find his sister's impassioned pleadings very compelling. His own decisive religious turning would take time to gestate, but Augusta had planted a seed. Though his religiosity was incubating, he *was* ready for "the Shop," as those familiar with the Royal Military Academy called it. Probably around the time of his fifteenth birthday, the name of Charles George Gordon, gentleman cadet, was entered into the Woolwich books.[8]

Some authors have depicted the four years that Gordon spent at the RMA as unhappy and lonely.[9] That is not true. While his feisty nature led him into some scrapes, most of these simply reflected the boisterousness typical of the Shop and any other contemporary institution of its kind. Gordon was independently minded and kept his own counsel, but these features of his personality were hardly extraordinary. What was more pronounced in the make-up of this particular cadet was a tendency to question or even to flout authority. One such incident at the RMA stands out in this regard. On being ordered, along with his fellow cadets, to walk and not run from the dining hall following meals, Gordon became impatient with what he viewed to be a petty rule. In response, he lowered his curly head and proceeded to use it as a battering ram, driving himself into the belly of the senior cadet assigned to keep order and knocking him backward down the stairs. For this impertinent transgression, he was nearly dismissed from the academy. At Gordon's hearing, the officious captain of cadets presiding, Frederick Eardley-Wilmot, remarked to Gordon that, "you'll never make an officer." Incensed that common dining-hall high jinks would elicit such caustic and exaggerated seriousness, Gordon dramatically ripped his epaulettes from his shoulders and threw them at the bullying captain.[10]

However, Gordon demonstrated a bit of the bully himself. In his final year, for instance, a fellow cadet accused Gordon of whacking him with a clothes brush and bruising his back. It may sound like an extreme action but at the time students were routinely birched for the slightest offense and the bruised cadet could have had an agenda because turning in a fellow cadet was rare. In any event, Gordon again found himself facing the wrath of the academy's authorities. They decided as punishment he would be put back two terms, delaying his graduation.

Gordon did not seem to mind his encounters with military officialdom. He simply focused on his studies. As he had demonstrated at Folland's House, Gordon was no scholar. Mathematics confounded him, as apparently did French.[11] But in mapmaking and in designing fortifications he showed real skill. As an aspiring engineer—known as a "sapper"—such skills marked him promisingly from the beginning of his military career. Some historians believe Gordon's intemperance and resulting rustication prevented him from gaining a commission in the more prestigious Royal Artillery. But that claim does not seem to be true.[12] Gordon desired service with the Royal Engineers, presumably because it played to his strengths. One might also surmise that a career with the engineers, as opposed to his father's in the Royal Artillery, was a demonstration of the independence characteristic of Gordon.

In any event, in June 1852 Gordon left Woolwich clutching his new commission as a second lieutenant in the Corps of the Royal Engineers. He was nineteen years old and ready to embark on a lifetime of service to the British crown and its slowly burgeoning empire. First he had to report to the Royal Engineers' Brompton barracks, located just outside Chatham, home of the famous naval dockyard.[13] Close to the barracks was the town of Rochester with the soaring presence of its impressive cathedral lined with memorials to fallen sappers, and where one day a similar memorial to Gordon himself would be erected.

Gordon quickly adjusted to life as a subaltern. He spent nineteen months at Brompton, soaking up the means and methods and esprit de corps of the Royal Engineers. Gordon developed his leadership skills and presided over companies of sappers and miners, who had the critical job in wartime of literally undermining the position of the enemy while solidifying that of their own. Gordon became highly adept at these skills during his time at Brompton. It was not all work and no play. He befriended an older officer, Lt. Col. Richard Jenkins. They went shooting for birds and small game together. In the absence of Gordon's father, newly stationed to command the guns at Gibraltar, Jenkins acted as an in loco parentis. The preparatory year and a half at Brompton went by quickly. In February 1854, Gordon was promoted to lieutenant and given his first posting: he would be assistant garrison engineer at Pembroke Dock, South Wales. The year of 1854 was pivotal in Victorian military history and Lieutenant Gordon, Royal Engineer (RE), was positioned perfectly to take part in it.

Perhaps the most unnecessary widespread conflict of the nineteenth century began in that year. The Crimean War would pull into its orbit the great powers of Britain and France in support of the Ottoman Empire against Russia. The British Empire was afraid that if the Ottoman Empire collapsed to the Russians, India would be threatened. During the course of the war's two-year execution, this "Eastern Question" would be placed squarely in the middle of international affairs.[14] For Gordon, whose first posting in a sleepy coastal Welsh garrison town was less than riveting, the outbreak of war in Crimea was a welcome potential call to action. What Pembroke Dock did not supply in frontline excitement it made up for in engagement of a different kind.

Gordon's latent religiosity began to emerge during his brief, ten-month stay in Wales. Integral to this fundamental spiritual change was the presence in his life of a young couple, Francis and Anne Drew. Captain Drew was an infantryman based in Pembroke and, together with his wife, was a fervent Christian. The early-nineteenth-century British evangelical revival was still very much in evidence at the time and the Drews represented it clearly.[15] They spoke freely of conversion, passed out earnestly written tracts, and lived the morally upright life characteristic of their co-religionists. Their impact on reviving Gordon's dormant Christianity was profound. Under the Drews' influence he seemed to experience a conversion and, as he recalled later, "I had a belief that Jesus was the son of God."[16] What before had been nominal for Gordon had become vital.

Inspired by the Drews Gordon read consistently throughout his stay at Pembroke. The Bible figured prominently in his spiritual studies, but so too did the well-known commentaries of the famous Scots Presbyterian theologian, Thomas Scott. Of special impact on Gordon was Scott's emphasis on St. Paul's theology. The Pauline aspiration found in Philippians 1:21 that "For to me to live is Christ, and to die is gain" seemed to have emboldened Gordon greatly, banishing from him forever the fear of death.

In later years, while either in the heat of battle or in anticipation of it, Gordon's fearlessness—at times manifested as an apparent welcoming of death—owed its animating spirit to Paul's teaching.

"I have turned over a new leaf," Gordon wrote happily to his overjoyed sister Augusta.[17] By his own admission, he was flooded with contentment because he believed wholly and sincerely that God was directing his life. Accordingly, in Pauline fashion, he resisted the world, the flesh, and the devil and was in a relentless struggle against temptation, especially the sins of pride and lust. Celibacy became a way of life for Gordon. He never married, nor, it seems, did he ever lose his virginity, no easy thing in a soldierly environment. He was committed absolutely to his awakened faith and it became his lodestar. His theological reading, as will be noted later, broadened in his later years, especially during the time he lived in Gravesend. But the course he embarked on under the guiding hand of the Drews at Pembroke would never vary. Gordon had become a soldier in two armies, the temporal and the spiritual, and he would do battle in both.

During the months that Gordon was solidifying his Christian faith in Pembroke, on the other side of Europe the conflict in Crimea had blown up to a full-scale war. As allies committed to the defense of the Ottoman Turks, Britain and France declared war on Russia at the end of March 1854. The fighting began quickly, much of it fierce and legendary, as at Balaclava in October of that year. It was there that the suicidal charge of the light brigade took place, immortalized by Lord Tennyson. "Into the valley of death," wrote England's Poet Laureate, "rode the six hundred." The charge was a bloody maw in which the Russian enemy was ultimately repelled. . . . As for the light brigade's commander, James Brudenell, 7th Earl of Cardigan, the infamy of this irascible man was sealed by the disastrous charge. Lord Raglan, the aging commander of the British forces in Crimea, did himself little honor in these foundational engagements of the war.

Meanwhile, Gordon was anticipating a call to the front from Pembroke and was greatly disappointed in the end of November when he was called to report not to Crimea, but to his old childhood home, the British base at Corfu. Undeterred, Gordon pleaded through a friend at the war office to be sent to Crimea. His superiors ultimately agreed—even then Gordon could be persuasive—and on December 3, 1854, he received notice that his orders were changed.[18] The next day Gordon left Pembroke and the Drews, whom he never saw again, for London and Balaclava. By then the Crimean War had evolved into a slugging match played out in frozen mud and craggy ice. None of this mattered to the zealous lieutenant, just shy of his twenty-second birthday. Off to Crimea he was, and not a moment too soon. Gordon arrived on January 2, 1855.

Crimea and Beyond:
Youthful Soldiering and Surveying

Great Britain was a satisfied, if not self-satisfied, country in the early 1850s. Queen Victoria was now past her youthful apprenticeship under her first prime minister, the paternal Whig, Lord Melbourne, and well into her reign. At the Queen's side was her beloved Albert, the German-born prince consort. Her majesty's government was led, beginning in 1852, by the impressively patrician George Hamilton Gordon, the 4th Earl of Aberdeen. His cabinet was full of similar worthies such as Lord Clarendon, the foreign secretary, and Lord Palmerston at the home office. However, as a coalition of Peelites and Whigs—more or less the antecedents of the later conservative and liberal parties—the Aberdeen government was not inherently stable.[1] Nonetheless, it was Aberdeen's prime ministership that led Britain into war in Crimea in 1854.

Aberdeen had the good fortune to come into office shortly after the six-month-long run of the Great Exhibition. Opening its doors in May of 1851, the commercial jamboree in London's Hyde Park featuring one hundred thousand exhibits was designed to show off the "Works of Industry of all Nations." Indeed, many of the exhibits were international, but the Great Exhibition was mainly a gigantic affirmation of the prowess and success of one hundred years of British industrial ingenuity.[2] Behind the

striking glass walls of former gardener Joseph Paxton's architectural marvel—dubbed the "Crystal Palace" by *Punch* magazine—everything from
hulking steam locomotives to delicate toast tongs could be found. In all,
more than six million people passed through its display halls, and thirty
thousand on the first day alone with seven hundred thousand more mill-
ing about outside. Praise for the Great Exhibition was wide and long, and
came from the queen herself: "This day is one of the greatest and most
glorious days of our lives," she wrote in her journal on May 1, 1851[3]

The British were on a fast gallop to the pinnacle of world power in
1851, or so it seemed. No other nation produced as much from its factories and mills; no other navy ruled the waves as did the descendants of
the mythic Nelson; and no other parliament gave its people the freedom
and liberty that Westminster did. Indeed, as Charles Dickens put it in
Dombey and Son: "Rivers and seas were formed to float their ships; rain-
bows to give them the promise of fair weather; winds blew for or against
their enterprises."[4]

The Crimean War provided a sharp jolt to Britain's self-congratulatory
mood. By the time that Britain and France declared war on Russia at the
end of March 1854, the crisis in Crimea, located on Russia's southern
flank, had been escalating for the previous seven years. The genesis of the
war was in late 1847 when the various Christian churches responsible for
maintaining Christ's birthplace in Bethlehem, the Church of the Nativity,
began to fight about access to the holy site. The crux of the dispute was
over control of the keys to the main door, which opens onto Manger
Square. The Orthodox and Armenian clergy had keys, but the Roman
Catholic priests did not. How this slightly ridiculous state of affairs developed involved age-old arguments and yellowing treaties. In 1847, maintaining the domestic tranquility of the multi-ethnic Ottoman Empire,
which controlled Palestine, was of considerable concern to the great powers
of Europe. Two years later, in 1849 when the French government of Louis
Napoleon, Bonaparte's nephew, decided to endorse the cause of the Catholic
clergy in Bethlehem, the diplomatic niceties of Metternich's long-estab-
lished, congress-ruled Europe began to unravel.

Napoleon III, as he became late in 1852, cared little for the devout
Catholic clergy residing in the Holy Land, but he was happily willing to
court favor with conservative Catholic groups in France to buttress his

shaky regime. He was also determined to disrupt continental alliances, which his countrymen widely believed had kept France in Europe's thrall since the ignominy of its lasting defeat under Bonaparte at Waterloo in 1815.[5] Neither Britain nor Russia nor the Ottoman Empire wished to see a revived France. The real threat to stability in the region came in February 1853 when the imposing Tsar Nicholas I of Russia sent an envoy to Constantinople to engineer a settlement of the Bethlehem dispute, and other related disputes. Russia had long viewed the Ottoman Empire as an obstacle to its own expansionist plans in the Mediterranean, and the tsar used the Bethlehem dispute to assert Russia's right to protect the Orthodox peoples who fell under Ottoman control. The sultan viewed the tsar's demand as an attack on Ottoman sovereignty.

Tsar Nicholas, in taking this aggressive tack, had misread Anglo-French enmity. They had long been archenemies, but with the Ottoman Empire's integrity being challenged and with the potential southern extension of Russian power, the British and the French found common ground. Over the next year, all diplomatic overtures failed and a general war looked inevitable. The Russians and Ottomans took up arms and, in November 1853 at Sinope on the Anatolian coast, an Ottoman fleet was attacked and destroyed by the Russians sailing from their main base at Sevastopol two hundred miles across the Black Sea. It seemed only a matter of time before the British and the French would declare war against Russia. In mid-March 1854 an alliance was duly signed between the unlikely allies of Britain, France, and the Turks. Two weeks later, Britain and France formalized declarations of war against Russia. The Crimean War had begun, having been initiated by nothing more notable than a ring of old keys.

Lt. Charles Gordon sailed into Balaclava about nine months after Britain and France declared war on Russia. Indeed, one would not have blamed Gordon for thinking he had arrived too late in Crimea and the real action was over. He had missed the storied charge of the light brigade, but for that he could be grateful and, after all, he was an engineer and would not have participated in it anyway. Later, Gordon, already displaying fatalism about death, told a friend that he had gone "to the Crimea hoping, without having a hand in it, to be killed."[6] Had he arrived earlier his fatalistic wish might have been granted. As it was, his desire to enter the everlasting kingdom would have to wait, although brutal Crimea would yet provide plenty of opportunities for a young man to die.

Gordon's arrival at Balaclava early in January 1855 involved steaming through the Straits of the Dardanelles, past Constantinople and Scutari— the latter where Florence Nightingale would become famous nursing the beleaguered British troops—and across the inky expanse of the aptly named Black Sea to the Crimean Peninsula. At its tip was Balaclava, a small and dirty port located just below the plateau where the Russian garrison town of Sevastopol sat.

Crimea was locked in the icy grip of winter when Gordon arrived. That fall, in addition to the Battle of Balaclava, serious fighting had occurred at Alma and at Inkerman. The British survivors of these costly victories were taken to the barrack hospital at Scutari, and one wonders if the wounded would not have preferred to be killed in action than face the appalling conditions of the military hospital. The place was fetid, a breeding ground for vermin, with sporadic heat and almost no cleanliness. Soldiers, some of whom had suffered horrible wounds, lay about untended. The lucky ones had found rickety beds on which to rest; the others did what they could to make a piece of the filthy floor passably comfortable. The dire situation was untenable, but it took the reporting of the *Times* of London to spur radical reforms. Florence Nightingale, at that time superintendent of the Establishment for Gentlewomen During Illness in London, read one of these reports and immediately sought to form a nursing service. Her request was met by a similar proposal the British government had simultaneously sent to her. She accepted immediately the position of superintendent of nursing in the English general hospitals in Turkey, was granted £1,000, and arrived in Scutari in early November. By Christmas, conditions had improved noticeably. The legend of the lady of the lamp was born.[7]

Gordon, young, excited, unhurt, and anxious to enter the fray, had flown through Scutari seemingly oblivious to the sufferings of many of his broken comrades. "Our wounded have everything that they want," he wrote in apparent ignorance, "and all comforts."[8] He was wrong, of course, although thanks to Nightingale and her fellow nurses the worst of the impact of disease and infection was over by the time Gordon reached Scutari. If Gordon were to die it would not be in the hospital at Scutari. Soon enough, however, a Russian marksman found him to be an inviting target: one day a bullet came close enough to him that he recorded being "struck by a spent ball."[9] But his luck held.

The skills Gordon had learned at the Royal Military Academy were put to good use. In anticipation of a spring offensive, he began to sketch the Russians' fortifications, as well as the defensive positions of the British. Sketching would be his main occupation for the next year and the experience of it turned him into a first-rate military designer. The camaraderie for which the army is famous filled the rest of his time. Two of Gordon's brothers, Enderby and Henry, were also in Crimea. In addition, he began a pair of lifelong friendships. One was with a polyglot Italian military interpreter named Romolo Gessi, who would reenter Gordon's life in a significant way twenty years later in Sudan. The other was with Garnet Wolseley, a young infantry officer destined to rise to the pinnacle of the Victorian army and who was charged with rescuing Gordon from Khartoum in 1884.

The highly fraternal nature of Gordon's time in Crimea included the opportunity to deepen his existing friendship with a fellow sapper from Woolwich, Gerald Graham. A bear of a man with a jaunty moustache, Graham would later win the Victoria Cross (VC), a decoration the queen created as a tribute to the acts of heroism in the Crimean War, and would be appointed to high command. In an otherwise starry career his greatest regret, he later said, was obeying orders to stay in Suakin, Sudan, rather than marching his men to Khartoum in the fall of 1884 to relieve Gordon. As for Gordon himself, Graham remarked with great disappointment that he had been "appointed Moses of a new Exodus, but with the Red Sea closed against him."[10] One of the enduring images of the siege of Khartoum is of Gordon standing alone on the rooftop of the governor's palace looking in vain for a slash of scarlet on the horizon, which would announce the arrival of British troops. He was an incessant smoker, his only obvious vice, a habit he had picked up in Crimea after being introduced to Turkish cigarettes, and he would surely have been smoking on the rooftop.

In Crimea, the expected spring push began in June and climaxed on June 18, 1855, a day of high symbolism to any British fighting man raised on a diet of Wellington and Waterloo. The British and the French were determined to breach the Russians' two stout fortifications at Sevastopol, Malakhov, and Redan. The expectation was that if they fell then the fortress itself would begin to give way, and the town's defenses would collapse. In the anticipation of a direct assault the allies began to weaken Sevastopol by lobbing incendiary bombs, known as "carcasses," over the walls. The result was a conflagration, followed by a general bombardment. In this manner, the French general, Aimable Pélissier, and his British counterpart, Lord Raglan, prepared for the final assault planned for June 18.

During this period of intense bombardment and withering fire, Gordon was hunkered down in a forward trench in an area known to the British as the Quarries. The work was loud and grubby and death was all around, but Gordon thought ten days of it would "finish this siege." The increasingly cowed Russians appeared, to Gordon at least, to be thinking the same thing. "Very downhearted" was how he described them in a letter home.[11] He was wrong. The Russians were not done yet. Fully aware of the intended allied assault, they brought up their reserves and used them to put up a fierce resistance. Indeed, the British attack on Redan was a costly failure, as was the simultaneous French assault on Malakhov. Sixty-two British officers and more than seven hundred soldiers were killed on what became a June 18 unlike that of the storied Waterloo.[12]

Throughout much of the fighting, Gordon was held in reserve to continue his sketching. Gigantic Gerald Graham, however, was in the thick of the fighting, where he performed the feat that won him the VC. Dodging a whirlwind of bullets, he carried his badly wounded commanding officer from the battlefield. No such heroics ensued for Gordon, and the immediate fight ended. Given the huge losses suffered and continuing Russian intransigence, Raglan decided against a second assault, as did French commander Pélissier, whom Raglan blamed for the day's failure. The French, he believed, had attacked with neither enough vigor, nor over a broad enough front, which would have had the effect of relieving the pressure on the British. "If the attack had been general," recorded Raglan, "the enemy's troops must have been scattered and there would have been no great mass anywhere and if confusion on their parts had ensued total defeat would have been the consequence."[13] He may have been right, although the French did not agree.

In any event, Raglan did not have much time to brood over the failure. Within a week of the repulse at Redan, he fell ill. Two days later, on June

28, he was dead. His quick passing was brought about by cholera and, some say, a broken heart.[14] Command of the British army then passed to the chief of staff, Gen. James Simpson. Meanwhile, much farther down the chain of command, Gordon was about to embark on an exhausting but exhilarating eight weeks, at the end of which the previously impregnable Sevastopol would at last fall.

Simpson would prove to be a weak and indecisive commander, even with the poor example of his deceased predecessor as a comparator. At least he was honest about it, though. "I am an unworthy successor to Lord Raglan," he wrote in July.[15] Fortunately for the British, Simpson's shortcomings—he was aging and pessimistic, and his health, at least in his own view, was fragile—were not of great significance to the war's outcome. In fairness to Simpson, he did not really want the job, but there was no viable replacement for him so he carried on with his duties stoically. Working in Simpson's and Britain's favor at this point was the fact the Russians were thoroughly tired of the war. The stomach for continuing the fight was leaving them, but that did not necessarily mean a quick end to the war. The new Russian tsar, Alexander II, had succeeded his deceased father in 1855 and was determined not to begin what proved to be a turbulent rule with a defeat. . . Consequently, the Russian forces dug in at Sevastopol with even greater certitude, forcing the allies to continue to bludgeon Redan and Malakhov, though in an increasingly spiritless manner. Boredom crept into the allied ranks, made worse by the prospect of having to endure another bitingly cold winter when all campaigning would cease and months of frostbite and privation would begin.

The tsar, not satisfied with the stalemate that now defined the war, urged his commanders "to do something decisive in order to bring this frightful massacre to a close."[16] That "something" took the form of the Battle of Chernaya in mid-August. The Russian soldiers, like their allied foes, were weak and dispirited, and their commanders achieved no element of surprise in the attack. The fight was nasty enough all the same, but the French repulsed the Russians fairly readily (the British were only lightly involved in the battle). The badly mauled Russians limped off the battlefield after suffering ten thousand casualties compared to fifteen hundred French casualties.[17] The terminal phase of the Crimean War had begun.

For Gordon, the weeks between the failed first assault on Redan and the success at Chernaya were spent in regular trench duty. Indeed, in what he described pithily in a letter home as "a bit tedious," Gordon spent thirty-four consecutive days in the trenches.[18] Life in the trenches, the "troglodyte world," as Paul Fussell called it memorably, is an awful thing in any war.[19] The dryness of summertime made it somewhat better for Gordon than it otherwise would have been, although one senses that weather or other environmental conditions did not have much of an impact on his ability to carry out the job at hand. Whether it was the hilly approaches to Sevastopol or later, the desert vistas of Darfur, Gordon never seemed to allow external forces to alter his resolve. In any event, the task before Gordon during the summer of 1855 in Crimea was to ensure that the British trenches remained in good repair and that his commanders were supplied with up-to-date intelligence on the Russian defenses. "If you want to know what the Russians are up to," the engineers at the front said, "send for Charlie Gordon."[20]

Both Gordon's physical doggedness and his skill for sketching were used well in Crimea, and he escaped unscathed. His habits were frugal and he seemed to relish the self-sufficiency required of soldiers at the front. In his letters home he reiterated that "comforts"—small care packages sent to the troops by their families that gained in popularity in Britain during the Crimean War—need not include him.[21] In most ways, the young Gordon relished the soldiering life and he highly anticipated the final assault on Sevastopol.

September 5, 1855, brought the expected allied bombardment in spectacular fashion. For three days the British and the French poured hot fire on the Russian redoubts that had proved so resistant two and a half months before. To Gordon, it was "one of the most tremendous bombardments ever seen," and it had the desired effect. On September 8 Malakhov was captured. The Russians defended it vigorously but were dislodged by the overpowering French.

At Redan, the British were not so fortunate. The attack was unsuccessful and by nightfall on September 5 the British retreated to await another push forward in the morning. Gordon's job was to sketch on the run, which he did while observing the heavy casualties (twenty-five hundred total) suffered by the British while the Russians continued to repulse them.

The expected morning assault never came, however. In light of French success at Malakhov and their inability to hit back successfully, the Russians decided to retreat from the south side of Sevastopol. The ensuing Russian evacuation was completed during the night and accompanied by blowing up their powder magazines, starting fires that raged throughout the city. To Gordon, Sevastopol's partial immolation was a "splendid sight, the whole town in flames."[22] By about eight AM on September 9 the pell-mell Russian evacuation across the bridge to the north side of the city was complete. Sevastopol had fallen. "We are at last in possession of the vile place," wrote Gordon.[23] Not quite, but the Russian abandonment of Sevastopol was the penultimate act in the Crimean War. The road to an allied victory and peace was close at hand.

Achieving a ceasefire with a peace treaty to follow, however, would take another six months. During that time, Gordon was assigned to the nine-thousand-man allied force going north to Kinburn on the Dnieper River, which successfully forced the Russian navy to withdraw. He then returned to Sevastopol and, with Gerald Graham, designed the shafts used to mine and blow up the destroyed city's dockyards and what remained of its arsenal and fortifications. Gordon was in his element with this task, although he admitted later he was not yet very good at it. But Gordon and Graham forged a lasting bond during the four months of entertaining pyrotechnics. "What a mess we made of that dock," Gordon later jokingly reminisced about Sevastopol to Graham.[24]

In March 1856, a month after Gordon saw the last charge detonated in the Sevastopol harbor, the war came to an end officially with the signing of the Treaty of Paris. Gordon prepared to leave the rubble-strewn city, but he did not know where he was going or what he would do. The young sapper had performed well during the previous fifteen months, and for it he was one of the few subalterns from the Royal Engineers awarded the French Legion d'honneur. One of the major provisions of the treaty was to survey the new frontier delineated between the Ottoman Empire and Russia. An international commission was being established on which Britain would have representation and Gordon, with his superior drawing ability and natural aptitude for map-making, was a perfect fit for it. By mid-March, he was duly ordered to join the British delegation headed by a fellow engineer, Col. Edward Stanton. Two months later he was in Galatz, a rather dreary but important port on the Danube River in what is today Romania. Using it as a base, he embarked on about a year's worth of border surveying, the main object of which was to keep Russia away from the vital Danube waterway. Such were the labors of relatively unknown subalterns.

The Boundary Commission, as the survey team was called, consisted of three Englishmen, one Frenchman, one Austrian, one Turk, and one Russian, along with an assortment of assistants. The ensuing months offered Gordon a multi-cultural feast. He met Bessarabians and Wallachians, Moldavians and more Russians, only this time not carrying guns. He drew maps and plans. He hiked, camped, and hunted; the latter was a reminder of his Chatham days. And in typical nineteenth-century style, Gordon shot to his heart's content. "I have killed about 100 head of game of different sorts this year," he reported home, although even that lofty number shows him to have been less enthusiastic about blood sports than most of his gun-toting contemporaries.[25]

The Danube survey was completed in the spring of 1857 and Gordon hoped to be going home. In Constantinople, however, he was ordered to join a commission surveying the new frontier in Armenia between Turkey and Russia. Though a little disgruntled, he had no choice. "Gordon must go," commanded the war office, and so he went. The countryside he encountered was buoying, however. Mostly mountainous, Gordon enjoyed a few adventures, including sliding toboggan-style down the face of towering seventeen-thousand-foot Mount Ararat, which Judeo-Christian tradition holds as the site where Noah's ark came to rest after the waters of the great deluge receded. By late summer, the unexpectedly enjoyable Armenian interlude had come to an end, and Gordon was able to go home to Southampton. He returned to a fairly new and elegant house, 5 Rockstone Place, not far from the center of the seaside town in which his parents had chosen to retire.

Gordon's stay in Southampton was followed by four months at the Royal Military College in Sandhurst, beginning in January 1858, and then, unexpectedly, by a return engagement surveying in Armenia. His work remained enjoyable for Gordon, as did the relative solitude that went with it. He also made good use of the emergent technology of the camera in Armenia, as he had earlier in Crimea, snapping evocative photographs of the people and the topography. His prowess as both surveyor and photographer brought him to the attention of the august Royal Geographical Society, which elected him a fellow that year.

The autumn of 1858 brought the end of his second Armenian assignment and twenty-five-year-old Lieutenant Gordon was uncertain of what his next assignment would be. One thing was clear, though: his fast-moving life thus far had left him uninterested in a conventional army career at home. "I do not feel at all inclined to settle in England and be employed in any sedentary way," he wrote his parents.[26] Such resolution meant, in the short term at least, staying in Constantinople with the prospect of joining the British team that was planning to erect a telegraph line from there to Baghdad, the capital of Mesopotamia. Alas, the expected order from the war office to do so never came through. Therefore, Gordon returned home once more to Southampton, spending the rest of 1858 and the New Year with his family.

It was only a matter of time before something would be directed his way. Gordon's stellar service in Crimea and good work on survey teams effectively guaranteed that he would not be overlooked on the long list of lieutenants awaiting appointment. When his appointment came the short wait was worth it: second adjutant of the Corps of Royal Engineers and adjutant of the Chatham depot. These may have been conventional appointments, but traditionally they were given to young officers of high promise. For Gordon, promoted to captain in April 1859, he would make the most of his second stint at Chatham even if it meant occasional concessions to what he considered to be trivial, rote military ceremony. "You will need," he wrote dryly to a fellow engineer, "at least eighteen pairs of spurs as you require them on all occasions. Sleeping in them is a nuisance at first, but you soon get used to them."[27]

Gordon took up his new position in May and held it for slightly longer than a year. The commandant at Chatham was Edward Stanton, his old chief from the Danube survey, so the atmosphere was warmly fraternal. Nonetheless, Gordon began to chafe at the restrictions to freedom and the barren routine of barracks life. Having spent most of the preceding four years engaged in various sorts of active service, Gordon found himself frustrated and bored. Stanton referred to Gordon an "ornament to the Service" in a letter to his father, but in Gordon's own mind, being stuck in Chatham was stultifying.[28] Luckily, he was not there long.

A war was underway in China, in which the British were becoming progressively involved, and it promised everything that prolonged languishment at the depot did not. His required year in Chatham almost complete, Gordon applied for active duty in China. The application was duly approved and in July 1860, he was on his way to the Orient, and, as it turned out, to fame.

China: To Wear the Yellow Jacket

Gordon, a world-conquering twenty-seven-year-old keen to be heading for action and away from desultory Chatham, had to endure a two-month passage to reach China. After crossing France he boarded a ship in Marseilles bound for Egypt. He traveled overland by train to Suez, a ride that included views of gangs of laborers digging the Suez Canal, which had begun construction five years earlier and would take another ten to complete. He then sailed through the Indian Ocean and up to Hong Kong, arriving in September. "Free trade" had become Britain's watchword in the Victorian era, and in the Far East no treaty port (a port open to western trade) demonstrated the concept more loudly than Hong Kong. Under British control since the 1840–42 Opium War and its concluding Treaty of Nanking, Hong Kong was one of seven treaty ports through which the "foreign devils" (as many Chinese, including the ruling Dowager Empress, viewed the British, the French, and other Westerners) were despoiling the country.

The British in China, like everywhere else in the world their ships had sailed, demanded to trade, and they were not discriminating about what composed the content of traded goods. Manufactured goods made in the smoke-belching factories in the English midlands and north satisfied part of the Chinese demand. But the greater portion of Britain's trade with China was in opium, grown in the high-yield poppy fields of imperial India, and at the root of a generation's worth of diplomatic unease and occasional open warfare.

In London, the newly elected liberal government headed by Lord Palmerston was more than willing to continue what its few critics thought to be saber-rattling policy. An overbearing grandee with a disdain for foreigners of any sort, who in this was much in line with the views of the cranky Dowager Empress, Palmerston was not about to trim Britain's trading sails in the face of objections from the execrable Chinese. If anything, they would be forcefully made to accept Britain's terms of trade. Gordon had arrived in China just in time to help with the forceful persuading.[1] But the situation in China seemed much less complicated than it was when viewed from London.

Under Palmerston, British policy in China maintained existing markets, opened new ones, and marginalized the competition. Ever since the swashbuckling Lord George Macartney, sent by the government of William Pitt the Younger, arrived at the court of the Manchu Emperor Qianlong in 1792, the British had considered China a natural partner for trade. In steady fashion, though punctuated by two nasty wars, a system of international treaties was forced upon the Chinese whereby Britain, as well as France and Russia, gained trading rights in China through the creation of treaty ports, such as Shanghai and Tientsin. In the perceptive observation of Jurgen Osterhammel, these ports had the effect of turning "large parts of China into an uncolonized extension of Empire."[2] The reigning Chinese Qing (or Manchu) dynasty grudgingly tolerated this Western irruption and by the middle of the nineteenth century had reached a sort of accommodation with it. Many Chinese, however, viewed the interventionist Westerners with their relentless demands for trade as harbingers of an impending cultural disaster and, falling back on a traditionally powerful Sino-centric isolationism, did their utmost to rid the celestial kingdom of the detested Western presence. Some of these people, such as the Dowager Empress, were members of the ruling class; many more, however, lay outside the walls of the "Forbidden City," the imperial palace in the capital of Peking. It was these people who made up the heart of the Taiping Rebellion, the bloodiest civil war the world has yet seen.

Lasting from 1850–64, the Taiping Rebellion, like most civil wars, was a complicated affair with a mixed pedigree and a diffuse impact. Indeed, calling it a mere rebellion does not really speak to the scale of the revolutionary upheavals it attempted to inspire. Originating in Kwangsi, one of the southernmost provinces in China, the Taiping Rebellion shook the old imperial order to its foundations and, in the estimation of its most comprehensive historian, Franz Michael, signaled "the beginning of the end of Confucian China."[3]

If revolution exists first in the mind of a single person, then in mid-nineteenth century China that person was named Hong Xiuquan (1814–64). A former schoolteacher and unsuccessful civil-service aspirant, Hong suffered a nervous breakdown in 1837 at the age of twenty-three. For the former farm boy, professional failures were sadly serial. Beginning in the early 1840s, however, Hong's developing semi-Christian religiosity began to coalesce into a strident millenarianism, defined by the long sought after promise of heaven on earth. Hong's initial exposure to Christianity had come at the hands of a tract-issuing, Yale-educated American missionary, Edwin Stevens, in the mid-1830s. Hong was living in his village home located near Canton, which, as a treaty port, had a substantial community of foreigners in its residential concession whose interactions with the local Chinese population both inside and outside the settlement's official boundaries were many and varied.[4] In 1836, Hong accepted a book of tracts from Stevens titled *Good Works for Exhorting the Age*. This simple compilation of missionary charges would prove to be the genesis of a strange concatenation of events, the result of which was the outbreak of rebellion in 1850.

The fourteen years following Hong's reception and reading of *Good Works* saw the development of a religious ideology that stressed a literal reading of the Bible, especially the New Testament. Meanwhile, Hong's continued failure in the examinations needed to win a place in the extraordinarily competitive civil service weighed on his mind. As a consequence of the pressure of this failure, his eventual psychological breakdown was spiked by hallucinations of great vividness and power. These hallucinations, or put more benignly, reveries, convinced him of a status and a calling far beyond the everyday, and certainly exclusive of the rather pedestrian concerns of the imperial civil service. In his heightened mental state Hong believed himself to be the younger brother of Jesus Christ, "God's Chinese son," whose dreams were divinely inspired and whose newly revealed task was to destroy, in his view, the manifestly corrupt Manchu dynasty and in its place introduce the vast Chinese population to the worship of the one true God.

During the 1840s, Hong proved highly charismatic and by 1850, such was his following that he founded the God Worshippers' Society in the village of Chin T'ien in Kwangsi province. The next year Hong proclaimed the Taiping "T'ien-Kuo," or Heavenly Kingdom of Great Peace. Hong's claim to be the son of heaven in a literal sense offered a fundamental challenge to the old order. Whereas Confucian, Buddhist, and Taoist dynastic cycles allowed for the existence of symbolic heavenly kings, or mythic deities, Hong's literalist claim undercut the mythological understanding of what it meant to be a son of heaven and portended a revolutionary break with the prevailing Chinese religio-political system.

The impact and growth of Hong's millenarian heavenly kingdom was swift. In early 1853, the then-militant Taiping converts conquered and held Nanking, the second city of the Chinese empire, killing thirty thousand people in the process, a portent of the long years of bloodshed to come. Peking was the ultimate goal, but as imperial resistance to the Taiping soldiers began to increase in light of their unexpected success, so too did the reality of a prolonged military stalemate. Hong's appeal, and that of the promised heavenly kingdom, existed on a number of levels: religious, political, economic, and social. As a movement, it comprised a mélange of influences, none of which is easily reducible. Therefore, it is difficult to call it, as some have, simply a peasants' revolt or a proto-nationalist uprising. The Taiping soldiers, with their long hair flowing defiantly in the wind, contrasting with the neatly tied braid of the Manchus, sponsored a rebellion that involved both of these things, and more.

Half a world away in London, the most important issue for the British government by 1860 was navigating the murky waters of both the Chinese imperial dynasty's continued resistance to trade, and the threatened stability caused by the fierce Taiping rebellion, which had, much to Britain's alarm, developed into a devastating civil war.[5] Specifically problematic was that the Treaty of Tientsin, negotiated the year before, had not yet been ratified by imperial China. In response, a combined Anglo-French force was preparing to march on Peking in a show of Western strength designed to force the hand of the Manchu dynasty in this regard. Such was the situation when Gordon arrived on the scene.

Sailing into Hong Kong in September 1860, Gordon found to his disappointment that he was "just too late for the fighting."[6] The Taku forts, which guarded the route to Peking, had fallen after having been stormed by the Anglo-French force. Therefore, an assault on the heavenly capital was imminent. Holding the rank of captain since the previous year, Gordon was made second in command of a company of Royal Engineers and prepared to join in the expected taking of Peking. On the way there, he passed through the major treaty port of Shanghai where imperial and Taiping forces had engaged in sustained and intense fighting. The irony was that the British were both defending and attacking imperial troops, depending on whether or not Taiping rebels were present. This three-cornered war was to no one's liking, except for the Taiping supporters, but it prevailed for a few months.

Gordon's disdain for the long hairs was almost immediate, as was his disappointment in local missionaries and their supporters back in Britain and the United States who hoped that Hong's inspirational, though admittedly aberrant, brand of Christianity might yet be set to rights with the acceptance of conventional faith. "By their works shall ye know them," and the legacy of the Taiping rebels, by now riven with infighting and assassination in the face of strong imperial counterattacks, was one of atrocity and starvation. The "cruel" Taiping soldiers with their "desolating presence," as Gordon described them, had found a new enemy.[7] Given Gordon's staunch Christian faith, this stance might not have been expected by the missionaries; but his mildly favorable early view of the Taiping rebels, based on a shared Christian faith, changed entirely when he witnessed their pitiless conduct of the war. In the meantime the imperial dynasty played for time, and to guarantee that foreign trading rights would continue in as uninterrupted a manner as possible, Gordon marched his subordinate band of sappers into Peking.

Initially, it was thought that the taking of the capital city would be a relatively quiet event. To this end, emissaries were sent ahead to negotiate a truce, but instead of their white flag being met in kind they were summarily and without explanation apprehended and put behind bars. In mid-October, the surrender of Peking came nonetheless. But Lord Elgin, the British commander, grew enraged when he found out that many of the emissaries and their accompanying escort of Indian troops had been tortured and killed. In retaliation, he ordered the emperor's summer palace burned to the ground. Accordingly, this spectacular example of Chinese architectural prowess and artistic achievement went up in smoke. Despite the cold-blooded provocations, Elgin's sense of required retribution was extreme and unjustifiable. Prior to the match being lit, the French and the British, including Gordon, looted the palace. He came away with various valuable items, including part of the elaborate imperial throne.[8] The timeless military practice of prize taking was one thing, but the burning to its foundations the Chinese equivalent of Versailles was quite another. For his part, Gordon thought it was wrong. "Vandal-like" he described the destruction of the palace, and he complained in a letter home that "it made one's heart sore" to be ordered to put the palace to the torch.[9] Acrid smoke choked Peking for two days as a result of the conflagration. Indeed, the whole episode smacked of unfettered power politics. Accordingly, the British and French got what they wanted: the Treaty of Tientsin was duly signed by the Chinese, helping to solidify what is usually called the "treaty century" in the diplomatic history of modern China, which would ensure its Western domination until WWII.[10]

In the aftermath of the taking of Peking, Gordon and his sappers were assigned the task of constructing living quarters for the British troops stationed in Tientsin to enforce, if necessary, the provisions of the newly signed treaty. This assignment stretched into an interminable eighteen months and the kinetic Gordon found activities to keep from succumbing to boredom. He took long exploratory rides on horseback; he hunted; he visited the Great Wall; and, in a foretaste of his post-China life in the quiet confines of Gravesend, he attempted to establish a charity. The latter did not work out very well, however, because on the day Gordon chose to distribute money to the local poor, some three thousand people arrived and in the crush and excitement eight of them were trampled underfoot and killed. Gordon contracted smallpox during his stay in China, but its impact was relatively mild and he survived easily.

A much more enjoyable feature of Gordon's protracted stay in Tientsin was the presence of family and friends. His soldier brother Henry passed through, and the commanding officer of the British contingent at the time, Brig. Gen. Charles Staveley, was the brother of Henry's wife, Rose. Gordon had known Staveley since the Crimean War and liked and respected him. Even better, though, was the presence in Tientsin of his great friend, Gerald Graham, and another brother-in-arms from the Crimean War, Garnet Wolseley, who was traveling along Britain's worldwide imperial trail. But even camaraderie began to pale in the midst of inactivity so nothing pleased Gordon more than when he was informed in March 1862 that he would be joining a force of one thousand British troops being sent to Shanghai. Taiping rebels threatened the treaty port and swift intervention, both foreign and imperial Chinese, was required.

Shanghai had been in peril for sometime. Half a year earlier, in September 1861, the city's foreign merchants and traders along with its Chinese bankers had banded together to raise and pay for an armed force to resist the increasingly harsh attacks of the rebels. This motley group of local ruffians led by foreign adventurers was nicknamed the Chang-sheng-chun, or the Ever Victorious Army (EVA). The foreigners called the group, more prosaically if less truthfully, the Disciplined Chinese Force. Regardless of its moniker, the EVA had achieved some success in small skirmishes with the rebels—hence the glorious name—but in the spring of 1862 a larger force was required.

A young U.S. buccaneer named Frederick Townsend Ward led the EVA. Born in Massachusetts in 1831, he had arrived in Shanghai as a penniless twenty-eight-year-old mercenary determined to find fame and fortune. He would be more successful in the first quest than the second, but offering himself to the treaty port's panicked merchants as just the sort of foreign expeditionary needed in its struggle with the Taiping rebels, Ward rapidly made a name for himself as a fearless fighter and a daring commander adept at the use of any modern weaponry on which he could get his hands.[11] In 1862, Ward's luck ran out and he was killed by the Taiping forces. He was succeeded by another rogue U.S. officer: the much less capable and apparently frequently drunk Henry Burgevine. Severe problems in command arose soon after Burgevine took charge.

At this rather inauspicious juncture, Britain chose to enter the escalating conflict more decisively. General Staveley, who was dispatched to head up the British force at Shanghai, sent for Gordon to command the Royal Engineers. Happy to leave Tientsin, Gordon arrived in early May 1862 and set to work immediately in a close reconnoitering of the Taiping defenses. The countryside around Shanghai and the Yangtze River delta was sprinkled with a number of small, walled towns connected by canals, many of which the Taiping rebels had overrun and occupied. In bunker-like style, they then held their ground against the imperial troops and the EVA. For the latter especially, breaking the defensive fortifications was proving to be immensely difficult and costly work. A change of tactics that would soon prove successful was at hand. Gordon was given the task of attacking selected fortified towns, and the first one that he and the troops took over was Tsingpu. From the deck of the small steamer *Hyson*, which would take on an important role in the coming months, Gordon first observed the town, and then on foot and under heavy fire, he moved to within one hundred yards of it to sketch its fortifications. Staveley regarded such daring as foolhardy: "I was so angry I would not speak to him, however much I admired his enthusiasm and devotion to duty," he later wrote of Gordon on this occasion.[12] Gordon's bold actions at Tsingpu were a harbinger of his semi-reckless style and they quickly began to work in favor of the EVA as well as the imperial government, which decided to significantly enlarge its support by deploying an additional ten thousand troops. For Gordon, the taking of Tsingpu was a turning point made more emphatic by the regimental band's playing "God Save the Queen" as the combined force of British and imperial troops—or "Imps" as he called them—marched uncontested through the main gate to secure the town.[13]

The taking of Tsingpu itself, however, was not something that translated very quickly into a significant advantage for the imperial government. The EVA was fighting relatively well, but under the unsavory Burgevine, its reputation for renegade-like behavior and rampant looting grew. To make matters worse, Burgevine viewed the Chinese with clear disdain and let them know it. Both the Chinese and the British hoped, therefore, to engineer his replacement. Early in 1863, they succeeded. In a fit of pique over what he regarded as the slow payment of his troops, Burgevine struck a Shanghai banker in the face, drawing blood with the blow. The assault would be the freebooting American's final transgression. Burgevine was unceremoniously relieved of command. The question then became, who would replace him at the head of the EVA? The top British official in Shanghai, Commissioner Sir Frederick Bruce, and the imperial governor and futai of Kiangsu province in which Shanghai was located, Li Hung Chang, had a plan. The new commander should be a "man of good temper, of clean hands, and a steady economist."[14] That is, he should be the antithesis of the recently ousted and unlamented Burgevine. Gordon, still out on survey, was held up as the one who fit best the description. Provided that Gordon wanted the job—and it fast became clear that he did—the appointment had to be approved first by the British government. Ordinarily, serving British officers were prohibited from taking an appointment under foreign command. Palmerston, though, approved the appointment for Gordon to take temporary service under the Chinese imperial government to command the EVA. On March 25, 1863, Gordon, not long after his thirtieth birthday and recently appointed brevet major, received official notification of his new position. The making of "Chinese" Gordon was in prospect.

The Ever Victorious Army, now more than at any time in its brief history destined to live up to its name, had a troop-strength of nearly four thousand, with members in all ranks. "G takes command. Told Footai [sic] eighteen months would see end of rebellion," is how Gordon confidently recorded the beginning of his time at the head of the EVA.[15] His timeline would prove to be about right. He began by inspecting his men, the artillery, guns, and ammunition. The EVA's collection of steamers and junks came under his watchful eye, as well. A week was needed for him to carry out this inventory. Fortunately for Gordon, the Taiping soldiers were past their peak in strength and their fighting spirit had begun to wane as the territory over which they were able to exert control was slowly shrinking. Moreover, owing to their murderous policies, the promise of newness and prosperity that Hong and the rebellion carried had proved false.[16] Gordon would use both of these developments to his advantage. But more important was his daringly shrewd decision to enlist captured Taiping prisoners in the serried ranks of the EVA. Playing on their hatred for the utopian musings of Hong and their despair at the horrific casualties of a civil war that was later calculated to have killed no fewer than twenty million and possibly as many as thirty million people, Gordon turned hundreds of the former enemy into EVA soldiers.[17]

Another brilliant move by the young commander was to take advantage of the network of canals that threaded their way through the Kiangsu province. To Ward and Burgevine, as well as to the imperial army, the canals had been seen as watery obstacles to be overcome rather than arteries to be followed in order to strike at the heart of the Taiping army's position. Indeed, the key to the EVA's success during the year and a half after Gordon became the commander was the degree to which Gordon mastered the use of the steamer, using a number of them to ferry supplies and troops to the point of attack, and outmaneuvering the enemy to do so.

A month after taking command, near the end of April, Gordon led the EVA against the Taiping soldiers at Quinsan. Located just west of Shanghai, about mid-way to the important rebel stronghold of Soochow on Tai Lake, Quinsan held a large arsenal of weapons and ammunition. Strategically, it was the key stepping-stone on the route to Soochow, which, it was thought, would break the rebellion if taken. Leading up to the attack on Quinsan, Gordon and his improved troops fought a successful battle at Chanza, which allowed the imperial flag to be raised in rebel-held territory. But Quinsan was the prize and everybody knew it. To reach it, however, an unexpected rebel victory over imperial troops at nearby Taitsan had to be reversed first. Within a week the EVA had done so and the town had fallen. Gordon's characteristically thorough reconnaissance had led to a pinpoint bombardment, which was followed by fierce close-range fighting. Gordon eschewed a weapon himself while leading from the front, however, content to push forward with a cigar thrust in his mouth and a two-foot long rattan cane slicing through the air. The decisive taking of Taitsan was a watershed moment in the establishment of both Gordon's charismatic leadership and his unconventional style of command. As bullets whizzed by his head, or scudded into the earth around his feet, the imperturbable Gordon continued to gain ground, seemingly oblivious to the Taiping soldiers' murderous fire. The long hairs, naturally, were unnerved by this enemy commander who seemed impervious to lead shot and whose only weapon soon came to be called the "wand of victory."[18] Not only did Gordon's stunning success and supremely confident manner begin to cow the Taiping rebels, they served as a salutary reminder to his own men—many of whom remembered with fondness the wild and wooly days experienced under Burgevine's command—of just who was in charge of the EVA. If any singular moment was the making of "Chinese" Gordon, the victory at Taitsan was it.

After Taitsan fell Gordon and his troops continued to Quinsan, which was taken and held by the end of May. Despite Gordon's ability to deliver victories and therefore prizes to his men, there were still those who continued to resent his systematic implementation of conventional military standards and procedures on what was essentially a force of irregulars. At Quinsan, for example, Gordon ordered a mutinous artilleryman shot, which in his estimation staved off a general uprising by the troops. Meanwhile, the ferocity of the attack at Taitsan, and allegations of brutality toward and summary execution of Taiping prisoners there, led to criticism of Gordon and the EVA in both Chinese and British newspapers. The longstanding sympathy of Christian missionaries toward Hong and the Taiping rebels was at play and demonstrated pointedly by the Anglican bishop of Victoria at Hong Kong, Dr. George Smith, who complained to the British government about the alleged unethical conduct of Gordon and the EVA.[19]

The criticisms were groundless given the circumstances, but they established in Gordon's mind the perception of missionaries interfering with military and political affairs. He would argue years later that missionaries and their meddling nature were behind some of his problems in Sudan. In the meantime, Soochow still loomed as the rebels' last major stronghold, and after settling his troops down at Quinsan (he enforced an unpopular order against looting), and rescuing some orphans, Gordon began to plot its fall.[20] "G. determines to attack Soo-chow," Gordon confided to his journal, "but on the same principle as Quinsan, viz. by cutting communications."[21] The rebel stronghold was well garrisoned with thirty thousand men so a frontal assault and pitched battle would have resulted in enormous, and probably pointless, casualties on both sides, along with an unavoidable concatenation of rape and pillage. Instead, Gordon bided his time through the debilitating heat and humidity of the Chinese summer while steadily isolating Soochow and cutting off its communication and supply lines.

Meanwhile, the disgraced Burgevine, annoyed by his earlier dismissal and plotting treachery in response, had raised a rogue force of mercenary fighters at Shanghai. He brought them to Soochow in the service of the Taiping rebels. Gordon, naturally, was amazed and furious at Burgevine's antics, although he calmed down enough to negotiate a ceasefire with the rebels. When Burgevine, most likely drunk, then decided to switch sides again and desert the Taiping soldiers, imperiling the temporary truce,

Gordon's patience snapped. He struck a deal with rebel leaders for them to hand over Burgevine. Gordon then sent him to the U.S. consulate in Shanghai with the hope that he would be expelled from the country: he was, but only to return the next year and cause further havoc. Burgevine would die in China, drowned in a boating accident in 1865 in what may have been a case of murder.

The removal of the unreliable and ridiculous Burgevine from the scene cleared the way for Gordon to attempt the negotiated surrender of Soochow. By December of 1863, the city was surrounded completely by EVA and Imperial troops. Inside Soochow's twenty-five-feet-high walls, the Taiping *wangs* (generals) conferred desperately with one another about their sorry predicament. In their deliberations, they seemed to have trusted Gordon implicitly, but the same could not be said of the imperial troops, who were ultimately controlled by the futai, Kiangsu's governor, Li Hung Chang. Nonetheless, negotiations proceeded and an agreement was reached. Its provisions included that Soochow must be surrendered fully and that the Taiping rebels, as a token of their submission to imperial authority, must cut off their long hair. If they complied, stated the futai, no acts of revenge would be taken against the wangs or their men. Unfortunately for the Taiping rebels, the futai lied. At the point of surrender the Taiping leaders were attacked, beheaded, and mutilated, and imperial troops were let loose to do their worst in the city.

Gordon, privy to the agreement but not its violation, was outraged by this manifest breach of honor by the futai, and in the white hotness of his anger vowed to seize and punish the governor. Using words such as "assassination" and "treachery" to describe the futai's actions, Gordon saw him as having betrayed the rules of war and caused the unnecessary spilling of even more blood.[22] Later, he would accept that the futai had been forced to deal with obviating circumstances, including a surly group of six wangs who refused to disarm as required by the terms of surrender.[23] But the whole episode was highly distasteful to Gordon for whom honor was a paramount virtue, and he then only hoped that the surrendering of Soochow would be the penultimate act in the seemingly endless civil war.

After Soochow was taken from rebel hands the imperial dynasty anticipated a complete victory. It was also swift to honor Gordon.[24] Still smarting from his sense of betrayal at the hands of the futai, however, he initially refused these overtures. Also, ever the soldier, Gordon knew there was still fighting to be done. Nanking, the Taiping capital and ultimate symbol of the rebellion, needed to be taken. Its eventual fall, however, would be reserved for the "Imps." As a matter of both honor and optics, Gordon and the EVA would not be asked to take any part in it. In the meantime, the march to Nanking meant securing victories over the last pockets of rebel resistance along the way: namely, Yesing and Liyang, which fell easily to the EVA and imperial troops. "The HOUR GLASS BROKEN," Gordon wrote emphatically in his journal, heralding the end.[25] But the war was not yet quite over. At Kitang, the Taiping soldiers mounted a spirited defense and succeeded in doing something that no one had yet been able to do: hitting Gordon with a bullet. The wand of victory did not protect him on the afternoon of March 21, 1864. He was shot in the thigh. The wound was not serious, and shortly thereafter he was back in the fray pushing towards Nanking. In May, Gordon fought his last battle in China, at Chang-chou. Two months later, in July, Nanking fell, overrun by imperial troops fighting alone. The long and staggeringly bloody Taiping Rebellion was over. Possibly from suicide, Hong died in June, succeeded by his son Tiangui Fu. But the "Young Monarch," fourteen-year-old Tiangui, died that November, executed by the renewed Chinese imperial state.[26]

After almost four years in China, the soon-to-be-promoted Lieutenant Colonel Gordon was ready to go home. The EVA, his instrument of victory, was disbanded, but the imperial dynasty insisted that its legacy be honored, and Gordon did not refuse the non-monetary rewards the dynasty offered. Giving an emphatic "no" to an offer of money, he readily accepted a mandarin's peacock-feather-trimmed hat, various ceremonial robes, two gold medals of victory struck to mark the occasion, and the high rank of *ti-tu*, or provincial commander in chief. Gordon prized the Emperor's Yellow Jacket above all, an honor restricted to a mere forty men and never before given to a foreigner. This esteemed reward for service, the grandest of the emperor's gifts, Gordon gladly accepted—some say even demanded—and modeled before packing everything up and heading home to England.[27]

In London, despite the ongoing protests by some missionaries and others about what they took to be the anti-Christian nature of the imperial and EVA enterprise against the Taiping rebels, the government chose to honor Gordon as well. Accordingly, he became Companion of the Bath. Meanwhile, the newspapers were fulsome in their praise of England's newest imperial hero, even though his description by some as a "soldier of fortune," would have been much better applied to Ward and Burgevine than to Gordon: "Never," enthused the *Times* in an editorial published in August, "did a soldier of fortune deport himself with a nicer sense of military honor, with more gallantry . . . than this officer who, after all his victories, has just laid down his sword."[28]

Gordon was uncomfortable with this kind of purple praise, however, and throughout the fall of 1864 he performed his last functions, dutifully collected his awards, and said his good-byes. A week prior to sailing from Shanghai he wrote to his mother "the individual is coming home but does not wish it known for it would be a signal for the disbanded to come to Southampton."[29] Maintaining this attempt at extra-familial anonymity, he signed the letter simply "Son." Gordon may have enjoyed being lauded by the Chinese, but he was not inclined to swap war stories with former colleagues should they discover his address in England. China was over, at least as far as he was concerned, and at the end of November his ship set sail for home.

Unbeknownst to Gordon, the inconvenience of a few ex-army colleagues potentially turning up at his parents' front door was nothing compared to the fame into which he was sailing. Fame would never sit easily on Gordon's soldiers, although later his critics would think otherwise. After four grueling years in China, he had certainly earned the accolades. However, there were those throughout his career who would attempt to diminish Gordon's key part in ending a brutal and protracted civil war by viewing him merely as a foreign gun for hire, conveniently forgetting that he was in the service of the Chinese emperor at the express permission of Her Majesty's government. Even more recent historians of the Taiping Rebellion have tended to underplay Gordon's role, one of them remarking factually but rather churlishly that the EVA "was by no means 'ever victorious.'"[30] Of course it was not, and no one, least of all Gordon, had ever assumed that the name of the EVA was to be taken literally.

However, to the Victorian public in January 1865, the month Gordon reached Southampton, meant the return home of the hero of the Ever Victorious Army. In a style typical of the man, Gordon had taken his time making the journey, the better to think about, one supposes, the only question important to the just-shy-of-thirty-two-year old: what was next in the life of "Chinese Gordon"?

The Years Between: Gravesend and Galatz

It took some time for Gordon to formulate an answer to the question of what to do next. The long sea voyage home helped, but after arriving in Southampton just after New Year's 1865 he seemed no closer to deciding on his next move than when he had left Shanghai two months before. After the heightened living of the previous four years, Gordon might have wished for an extended period of relaxation and reassessment. Such was the result of a lengthy stay with his parents along with the writing up of his journal from the China campaign. The state of his health, too, was at least a small concern. After years of mostly rough living in the Orient, it is a wonder that his complaints were not greater than the one that he did register: "I am so very seedy from liver and ague."[1] Clearly a man of the age in describing himself in this way, Gordon had survived his China sojourn remarkably well. In the meantime, he tried hard to enjoy a bit of the feting and fussing over his accomplishments in China that seemed to greet him at every turn. As his anonymous letter home to his parents on the eve of his leaving China suggests, he was genuinely uncomfortable in the spotlight. Moreover, it would seem that his attempts to avoid it were not induced by false pride: "I hate and abhor being complimented or having speeches made," Gordon remarked to a friend.[2] He did his utmost to avoid both compliments and speeches, although when the Royal Engineers honored him with a banquet he was "highly gratified."[3]

One place where approbation was not universally forthcoming, however, was at his family's home, Rockstone Place. His father always had been less than wholly impressed with Charlie's Chinese service. Old General Gordon was of the opinion that serving British officers should not put themselves under foreign command. Gordon's time in China was approved and sponsored by the British government, but the senior Gordon, now ill and dying, was skeptical nonetheless.[4] His father, mind unchanged on this point, died in September. His death caused Gordon intense grief and sparked a period of close introspection. That same month, partly as a way to deal with his bereavement, he decided to forgo his remaining six months of leave and accept a new post: commanding officer of the Royal Engineers at Gravesend. Located on the Thames estuary near the river's mouth, Gravesend was a sleepy tidal town. Given his subdued state of mind, Gordon was glad for its relative somnolence. He would be left alone in Gravesend, alone with his thoughts and able to mourn his dead father in whatever way he chose. He later remembered this period in his life: "I used to walk out to Chalk [a nearby village] in the afternoon and go into the churchyard and think about my father, and kick the stones about and walk back again."[5]

After the excitement of China, the move to Gravesend might have seemed overly pedestrian, too stark a contrast from the stirring martial scenes of Taitsan and Quinsan. But Gordon customarily attended to the work at hand, busying himself with the construction of a series of forts designed to guard the riverine approach to London. However, his contrarian view of things came to the fore early in his stay at Gravesend. Despite his position of command he had little use for the new forts, thinking of them simply as too-costly barracks and next to useless against a determined invading army (still anachronistically assumed to be the French). When the commander in chief of the British army, the Duke of Cambridge, visited Gravesend and commended Gordon for the good work being done on the fortifications and on one gun battery in particular, Gordon replied candidly: "I had nothing to do with it, sir; it was built regardless of my opinion, and, in fact, I entirely disapprove of its arrangement and position."[6] Never one to mince words, Gordon's outspokenness and impatience with officialdom had been reinforced by his years in China and would be a defining feature of his personality for the rest of his life.

At Gravesend, Gordon's daily official work occupied him only until the early afternoon. What could have been a recipe for prolonged boredom and excruciating introspection instead became an opportunity for extensive charitable works. From 8:00 AM until about 2:00 PM, Gordon flew from site to site, monitoring construction of the forts and batteries, ensuring that building supplies were adequate, and that dutiful workmanship was done. Like many of his Victorian contemporaries—W. E. Gladstone, whose life would intersect later with Gordon's so profoundly, perhaps being the best example—Gordon abhorred the waste of time.[7] Ultimately, he believed, the Almighty would hold him accountable for each day and hour of his life. "Only one day t'will soon be past," went the somber contemporary reminder, "only what's done for Christ will last." Increasingly, Gordon began to act in accordance with this injunction.

Ever since his religious awakening at Pembroke Dock, Gordon had attempted to live soberly and spiritually, and his essentially evangelical faith introduced to him there by his friends, the Drews, was an exacting tutor. The searchlight power of evangelicalism to probe and expose the hidden places of the heart was one of its defining features.[8] Gordon, given to brooding and self-examination by nature, was an ideal anvil on which to hammer out a "new creature in Christ," as the apostle Paul would have it.[9] The desire to live out his faith in practical ways, the idea that faith without action is dead, animated him strongly. Gravesend, like most Victorian towns, was an amalgam of rich and poor, a mix of the High Street and the back street, and there were myriad churches busily engaged in dispensing charity to ameliorate the grossest of social disparities. Gravesend had a workhouse offering residence to those who could not support themselves, and it was the main recipient of government charity in the town. Gordon directed his charitable energies toward the workhouse and its infirmary. He also opened his own home, Fort House, to anyone wishing to stroll through the ample gardens and view the harbor below. He even set aside plots of ground within the gardens for any of the town's poor interested in cultivating their own vegetables. Despite all of these activities, however, nothing seemed to quell the restlessness of his mind and spirit.

Gordon carried on in this way for some time. His official duties engaged him for half the day, followed by a round of charitable activities. Increasingly, though, the latter became desultory. He felt inadequate for the task and lacking in the committed and genuine Christian frame of mind. Some historians refer to his befuddlement as a representation of what Gordon called "Agag," his conflicting desires for action (and perhaps fame) and a life of humility and service.[10] He found himself, as in the 1850s, in spiritual crisis. Writing to Augusta in the late spring of 1866, Gordon pinpointed the problem this way: "The secret of our troubles is want of love to God. . . . I am sure it is our besetting sin."[11]

A vexatious summer followed, but by autumn an answer had come in a medium common to evangelical Christians. Biblical text spoke powerfully to Gordon and cast out all of his doubt: "Whosoever shall confess that Jesus is the Son of God, God dwelleth in him, and he in God."[12] Ruminating upon this passage of Scripture and accepting the principle that God dwells in each believer proved an immediate antidote to his spiritual malaise. Gordon had been awakened to the idea that God truly lived within him and transformed his body into the temple of the Holy Spirit. This recognition turned out to be the final great spiritual moment of his life, and it spurred him to deepen his commitment to the poor and dispossessed of Gravesend, and to do so with a glad heart. "God did not redeem us to be feeble and weak," Gordon wrote soon after his epiphany, "but He redeemed us for His service, to joy in Him, to know Him in His thick darkness."[13]

Gordon enlarged his charitable commitments. He was free with his money and his time. He wrote a Christian tract, which he distributed around Gravesend, and he began to read more broadly, including *The Imitation of Christ* by Thomas à Kempis and *Christ Mystical*, a standard work of seventeenth-century devotion written by the Church of England bishop, Joseph Hall. He even began reading the works of the former Anglican worthy turned influential Roman Catholic, John Henry Newman, especially his well-known mystical poem, "The Dream of Gerontius."

Cementing into place this new charitable thrust and his deeper reading was the development of a friendship with a local couple akin to that which Gordon had made with the Drews in Wales. Unlike that relationship, which did not continue much beyond his brief posting in Pembroke, this one would last the rest of his life. Frederick and Octavia Freese lived just outside Gravesend in the village of Milton. They had a young family, were devoted Christians, and, after Octavia had met Gordon at the local branch office of the Religious Tract Society, became fast friends of Gordon's. At first, the Freeses had no idea that the Gordon they knew was the Gordon of Chinese fame. A few weeks into their friendship, the topic of China came up in conversation and, having mentioned that he had traveled there, Gordon was asked if he had witnessed anything of the Taiping Rebellion. "I should think I did," he expostulated, "why it was I who put an end to it!"[14] One might forgive him for his flight of hyperbole; after being referred to constantly in the press for almost two years as "Chinese" Gordon it may have been inconceivable to him that the well-informed Freeses were ignorant as to his identity. In any event, the friendship blossomed—especially between Gordon and Octavia Freese—and for the next five years the lives of all of them were deeply entwined. The Freese's young son, Eddie, was Gordon's favorite, and as recalled by the grown Eddie many years later, the sentiment was mutual: "I remember well the feeling of the air of love and indefinable mystery that seemed always to surround him. . . . We used to see him nearly every day and his wonderful influence seemed to pervade our lives."[15]

Equally important to Gordon was his growing charitable work, which came to include the operating of a night school for disadvantaged boys out of some of the unused rooms in the overlarge Fort House. His school for "scuttlers," as he affectionately called them, began with the sons of his housekeeper, but soon expanded to include many more boys. Along with the help of a few friends, Gordon endeavored to give these boys—in various stages of poverty, ignorance, and ill health—a rudimentary education. He also sought to place the older ones in jobs, many of them going to sea as a result. In addition, upon the recommendation of William Freese, Gordon became a committee member of the local Ragged School, which, in those last years before primary education became state mandated in 1870, was part of a national network of schools designed to educate the poorest and most disadvantaged British children. Once a week, Gordon arrived at the school and instructed the gathered boys and girls. The work was not easy, but Gordon seemed to thrive doing it. His evident enthusiasm and care for the children and adolescents in his charge was reciprocated. "He made me feel, first of all," recalled one of them years later, "the meaning of the phrase, the Goodness of God. Goodness became to me, through Gordon, the most desirable of ideals. . . . We were under the spell of Gordon's personality. We lived in the magic of his mystery—enchanted."[16] Less effusively stated, though presumably as heartfelt, was the misspelled graffito scrawled on a wall near Fort House. It read simply, "God Bless the Kernel."[17]

In a later Freudian age, Gordon's motivations for spending so much time with young boys were attributed to subconscious homosexual desire.[18] Even in the recently published *Oxford Dictionary of National Biography* he is described, with evident ambiguous intent, as a "boy lover."[19] However, no evidence exists of any impropriety in his dealings with the youth of Gravesend.Gordon, as noted earlier, had decided as a young man to remain unmarried. His comment that "married men have more or less a cowed look" is chauvinistic but also reflective of his choice to remain single. Like anyone else, Gordon in his youth had experienced the powerful effect of his own budding sexuality: "I wished I was a eunuch at fourteen," he wrote later in life to a friend.[20] Even so, suggesting that his impetus for charitable work among the poverty-stricken boys of Gravesend was sexual in nature represents the groundless speculation sadly representative of a generation introduced to Gordon by the loose musings of Lytton Strachey.

The combination of his official work and private charity made Gordon's years in Gravesend "the most peaceful and happy of his life," recalled a fellow Royal Engineer, who was stationed with Gordon in Gravesend.[21] His friendships and associations had deepened, and his restless spirit had found peace in the belief that God dwelt within him. Despite Gordon's sense of personal fulfillment, he was nevertheless a career soldier for whom action on the frontline was a way of life. Gravesend was a pleasant place but in military terms it was a backwater, and Gordon kept his eye on the possibilities that lay elsewhere. In 1867, Gordon hoped he would be named to an expedition to Abyssinia (present-day Ethiopia) to rescue British diplomats stationed there from the clutches of its renegade emperor, Theodore. It was not to be.

Meanwhile, his mind returned constantly to China, and he thought he might be called back into service there. While in Gravesend, he had ensured that as many of the officers and men who had served with him in

China as he could locate were duly rewarded with the medals that the Chinese government had struck in honor of the Ever Victorious Army. For many of them the honor was a posthumous one, which for Gordon, concerned as he was with contacting their next of kin, made the task urgent so as to lessen their bereavement. Sometimes it proved impossible to track down relatives of the deceased officer or soldier, but when he did so successfully he would send the medal accompanied by a personal note, the response to which was usually immediate and touchingly emotional.[22] "I beg leave to state," wrote the grieving mother of one dead officer, "that I received this morning the cherished memento of my Dear Son: and we the Father and Mother of the late Capt. George Smyth tender our most sincere and heartfelt thanks to Colonel Gordon for his courtesy and kindness in forwarding the medal, and we thank you most kindly for the favourable and affectionate manner in which you speak of his conduct."[23]

Gordon, however, was not to see a second engagement in China—at least not for the time being. His next assignment would keep him in Europe and return him to a life akin to the one that he had led fifteen years earlier. He was going back to the Danube. In 1871, the Gladstone liberal government made Gordon the British representative on the Danube Commission. As far as Gordon was concerned the post was hardly ideal but after six years in Gravesend, the seasoned thirty-eight-year-old lieutenant colonel was ready to leave, even if it meant a return to the well-plowed ground of his youth without troops to inspire. He said his heartfelt good-byes and in October departed Gravesend for his former base of Galatz.

The main Danubian port in Romania, Galatz remained much as it had been when Gordon had seen it in 1857. A "straggling town," he described it, the place did not do much for Gordon's less-than-exuberant state of mind.[24] He was even less impressed with the workings of the Danube Commission, on which he was normally the only resident European commissioner and therefore was responsible for most of the work. However, he was busy, only on those occasions when his fellow commissioners gathered in Galatz to make recommendations for safe navigation on the Danube and on the right of all nations to unencumbered passage along it. For Gordon, the only pleasant part of the job was renewing his friendship with an old Crimean colleague, Romolo Gessi, then living in Romania's capital city of Bucharest.

The kind of bureaucratic work that the Danube Commission demanded of Gordon at this stage in his life was stultifying, so he sought respite by leaving Galatz as frequently as possible and traveling extensively through the countryside. Almost a year into the deadening assignment, the pace quickened unexpectedly, and Gordon's spirits rose accordingly when he was sent to Crimea in the summer of 1872. Happy to be returning, if only briefly, to the site of his military coming of age, Gordon had been asked by the War Office to assess the state of Britain's Crimean War cemeteries, a task he duly performed. While in Crimea he received an unexpected invitation to a dinner being given by the British ambassador to Turkey, Sir Henry Elliott, at his summer residence on the Bosporus outside Constantinople. Nubar Pasha was also at the dinner table on that September evening. Nubar was in the service of the Khedive Ismail, the ruler of Egypt under the Ottomans and Sudan, its vast suzerainty to the south. Their meeting would change Gordon's life.

Nubar was an Armenian Christian, part of a substantial minority within the Turkish Ottoman Empire that would come to suffer greatly under the sultan's rule and become the focus of Gladstone's last great moral and political crusade in the mid-1890s. A generation earlier, Nubar was both prime minister and foreign minister of Egypt, and when he met Gordon he was looking for a suitable successor to the governor-general of Equatoria, or southern Sudan, Sir Samuel Baker. An intrepid, adventurous Englishman, Baker had spent the better part of thirty years on the British imperial road. Baker had explored, traveled, and lived in Ceylon, Central Africa, and Egypt, and in the service of the Khedive had done his best to open up the still-mysterious Nile route to the heart of the African continent. In exchange for the princely sum of £10,000 annually (approximately U.S. $1 million) for four years, Baker was charged with "the establishment of legitimate commerce throughout these countries, [which] will be a great stride forward towards future civilization, and will result in the opening to steam navigation of the great equatorial lakes of Central Africa and in the establishment of a permanent government."[25]

These formidable tasks had proven beyond even the hearty Baker's reach, especially "the establishment of legitimate commerce," a polite euphemism for stamping out the ubiquitous and mostly Arab-run slave trade. The Khedive hoped a new governor-general might have better success and awaited the expiration of Baker's lucrative contract in 1873. In the meantime, Nubar was working hard to find the right replacement for him. After a lively dinner conversation about Equatoria at the British ambassador's summer retreat, Nubar began to think that Gordon might be his man.

After returning to Cairo, Nubar's decided to trust his hunch but waited for Baker to formally complete his term and vacate Egypt before acting on it. During that time, Gordon visited home where his mother lay ill and would die within a year. Early in 1873, Gordon had not heard from Nubar and returned to Galatz. Explaining to a friend with evident understatement that it "never did suit me to be here," he determined to resign his commissionership, although without a formal offer from the Khedive he did not know where to go.[26] The Khedivial regime's wheels began to turn faster during the summer and in early September the British government informed Gordon that he was wanted by Egypt as the governor-general of Equatoria. A leave from active service in the British army was granted. In October the appointment was formalized. Gordon was going to southern Sudan as governor-general accompanied by big expectations for success against the slavers.

That same autumn, Samuel Baker returned to England where he was feted by the Royal Geographical Society and by royalty, and retired to a grand country house in Devonshire. Although his four years in the service of the Khedive had made him wealthy, his impact on southern Sudan had been negligible. However, he did not see it that way: "The White Nile," Baker wrote triumphantly, "for a distance of 1,600 miles from Khartoum to Central Africa, was cleansed from the abomination of a traffic which had hitherto sullied its waters. Every cloud had passed away, and the term of my office expired in peace and sunshine. In this result I humbly trade God's blessing."[27]

Despite the brief adulation displayed upon his return home, few with any real knowledge of Sudan took Baker's self-serving exaggeration at face value, least of all Gordon, who remarked: "After a study of Sir Samuel Baker's expedition, gathered from his letters in the papers, I think he was guided by a wish to glorify himself."[28] Gordon was probably right. As for his own motivations, he had no illusions about ending the slave trade either easily or quickly. "Born in the people, it needs more than an expedition to eradicate it," he wrote presciently to Augusta on the eve of his departure.[29]

Gordon turned forty-one years old on January 28, 1874, which was also the day he left for Egypt and Sudan. That day news of the lonely death of David Livingstone reached England. The great missionary-explorer had died the previous May, and his sun-baked body would be returned from Africa for burial at Westminster Abbey in a funeral epic emblematic of the Victorian age. As for Gordon, he was headed the other way. "Goodbye," he wrote simply on a postcard sent to the Freeses, along with the notation, "Isaiah 35," and a sketch of a rising sun and a palm tree.[30] "The wilderness and the dry land shall be glad," begins the Old Testament prophet's chapter, "the desert shall rejoice and blossom." And with that, Charles Gordon was gone.

Sudan I: Exploration, Slavery, and Abolition

Sudan, the country to which Gordon attached himself in 1874, was a forbidding and hostile place. Its fortunes were tied inextricably to Egypt, whose own suzerainty of Sudan had been kept in place by the overlordship of both Britain and France. The French had arrived first in the eastern Mediterranean in 1798 when the Napoleonic navy had sponsored a brief invasion of Egypt. Beaten decisively by the Royal navy under Lord Nelson later that year at the Battle of the Nile, Napoleon limped home to France in 1799. The occupation dragged on for two more years until British troops finally expelled the French in 1801. Thus began a long period of British influence, primarily economic, that was mediated first through Muhammad Ali and then his successor khedives acting under Turkish control. "Here was a country . . ." as Lord Alfred Milner, the archetypal British imperial proconsul would describe the Egyptian situation later on, "which during the last half-century had been becoming ever more and more an appanage of Europe, in which thousands of European lives and millions of European capital were at stake, and in which of all European nations Great Britain was, by virtue of its enormous direct trade and still more enormous transit trade, the most deeply interested."[1]

In 1869, the importance of Egypt to Britain and Europe was magnified greatly by the opening of the Suez Canal, which proved a boon to worldwide British trade, as it diminished travel time along the vital passage to India by two-thirds. Strategically, North and Central Africa had emerged as preeminent among British geopolitical concerns because of its apparent link to the canal and therefore to India's security. The mystery of the Nile's headwaters had been solved after a series of celebrated and successful expeditions undertaken to find the great river's source. Indeed, David Livingstone's final poignant peregrinations in Central Africa were in search of an answer already found and then confirmed by his contemporaries John Hanning Speke, Richard Augustus Grant, and Samuel Baker.[2] The intense drama of the Nile quest had passed by the time of Gordon's arrival at Khartoum in March 1874, but the Great Lakes of Central Africa, while confirmed as the genesis of the 4,200-hundred-mile-long Nile, were not well known. Surveying the Nile and the Great Lakes that lay at its head was Gordon's immediate task at hand.

Gordon had come out to Sudan through Cairo. There he had met the khedive and surprised him by rejecting the enormous £10,000 annual salary of his predecessor Baker. "What an extraordinary Englishman!" exclaimed Ismail. "He doesn't want money."[3] Gordon thought £2,000 per year would be sufficient for his needs, and carrying the official *firman*, the executive order, announcing his name and title—in his view far too grandly—as His Excellency Gordon Pasha, Governor-General of the Equator, he set off southwards. Accompanying him were some recently acquired staff members, including Romolo Gessi, who had heeded Gordon's call and come from Budapest to Egypt, as well as a young U.S. ex-army officer Charles Chaille-Long, whose dyspeptic and inaccurate recollections of his brief time on Gordon's staff later became the main source of information used by Lytton Strachey to create his false portrait of Gordon in *Eminent Victorians*.

Gordon's arrival in Khartoum was met with a party thrown by the governor general of Sudan, Ismail Pasha Aiyub. Food and drink were offered for guests' enjoyment, as were scantily clad local Nubian dancing girls. The gyrating and excessive drinking were not to Gordon's taste, so he left the party early and began immediately to make final plans for his forthcoming almost seven-hundred-mile expedition up the Nile as far as

Gondokoro, the capital of Equatoria, and the lakes region beyond. In the meantime, protocol demanded that he throw a reciprocal party for Aiyub. Using stores mostly leftover from Baker's time—including champagne and fine china—Gordon grudgingly did what was required of him. The rest of his week in Khartoum was comprised of gathering supplies, outfitting the steamer *Khedive*, which both then and later would do yeoman service along the river, and composing and issuing a decree outlawing armed marauders and gunpowder in Equatoria. These two prohibitions, along with an accompanying one making trading in ivory a government monopoly, made it clear that Gordon was out to hit hard against the slave trade. The terror-filled slave hunts could not operate without gunpowder. And if ivory was under strict government control, no slaver could hide behind its dubious legitimacy.

Proceeding up the Nile towards the Sudd, a large area of tangled, thick floating vegetation that made navigation very difficult, Gordon reached Fashoda—later to be the site of the surrender of the French and their imperial ambitions in North Africa to the British in 1898. Changing steamers to the faster *Bordein* he reached Gondokoro, his new headquarters, in mid-April. A squalid little bush town, Gondokoro would serve as the launch pad for Gordon's anti-slave-trade campaign for the next two years, an endeavor that was already showing signs of being undercut by Aiyub back in Khartoum. The khedive's desire to end the slave trade was genuine, but the economic stakes were too high closer to the scene of the action and this meant that Aiyub—who benefited personally from the trade—made a concerted effort to frustrate Gordon in his work. The diplomatic niceties on Gordon's arrival in Khartoum were a thing of the past, and it became clear to Gordon that Aiyub would do all that he could to weaken his position. "The great object of my foe Ismail Pasha Aiyub," he wrote later to Augusta, "was to keep me in this state and my great object was to break out of it."[4]

During these early days in Equatoria, the main problem for Gordon was the irregularity of shipments of supplies—chiefly caused by the interfering handiwork of Aiyub—and the serial sickness of his crew of subordinates. Gordon was so hamstrung by Khartoum that he decided on a new course of action: "I could not be continually writing to the Khedive about the non-supply of things and money;" he wrote in September 1875, "it would have worn me and every one out. Now I am quite independent, raise my own revenue and administer it."[5] As for his ailing men, afflicted mostly with malaria: "Never let the mosquito curtain out of your sight," Gordon implored them, "it is more valuable . . . than your revolver."[6] Nonetheless, Gordon's plan to establish a series of stations along the Nile from Lado in the south, above Gondokoro, to Dufile near the lands ruled over by Mtesa, the *kabaka* (king) of the Buganda (today's Uganda), continued apace. He reasoned that these stations would prove to be outposts from whence the slave trade could be broken up incrementally. His work quickly became that of an explorer because his ascension of the river was taking him into an area of Central Africa not yet much traversed by Europeans. The hope was that the western branch of the Nile flowed out of Lake Albert, although since no European had been that way, it was merely a guess.

The hardships and privations of this endeavor were constant: sick men, a suspicious local population, an unforgiving river that served up difficult-to-navigate cataracts with deflating regularity, and officials (mostly Egyptian) who were most often both inept and corrupt. At one station, for example, located about midway between Lado and Dufile, Gordon recorded the following scene in September 1875: "Fancy my horror at hearing to-day that the officer left in charge at Kerri had, while the taxes were being collected, allowed some hundreds of armed natives to enter the station. I fined him three months' pay (£12) and reduced him to the ranks. The natives had sent in a great supply of merissa [local beer] and the men were half-drunk. These are the sort of officers I have."[7]

For Gordon, a close-up view of native Sudanese life along the Upper Nile, and the havoc wreaked upon it by the slave trade, was appalling. He described the scene in a letter to Octavia Freese: "It was and is the wholesale depopulation of districts which makes slavery such a curse . . . A fair and properly conducted emigration would be the best thing for these parts . . . It will be a very long time before much can be done . . . the climate is against it and there can be no trade for they having [sic] nothing to exchange for goods. Poor creatures they would like to be left alone."[8]

Unlike most of his men, some of who died and others of whom had to be invalided to Khartoum or Cairo, Gordon was able to stay reasonably free of illness during this period, although the rigors of the passage south were commented on repeatedly in his correspondence. "This is a horrid climate," he wrote to Augusta early in 1876. "I seldom, if ever, get a good sleep."[9] One of his men, Chaille-Long, wrote later that Gordon's method of coping with the climate and the demands of the campaign was to take to his hut for long periods of time, during which he would drink and ruminate, only to emerge in an agitated state and then excoriate his subordinates for some alleged misdeed. Strachey was to use Chaille-Long's recollections of the Equatorial campaign as the basis for his profile of Gordon. None of what Chaille-Long wrote was corroborated by anyone else on Gordon's staff. It would seem that early on in the expedition Gordon had found the American to be vain and nearly useless, concerned mostly with his position as a surreptitious informant for the khedive. Not long after meeting him, Gordon wrote to Augusta that Chaille-Long was "a regular failure," a view that he maintained and one that, in characteristically blunt style, he made clear to Chaille-Long himself.[10] Hence, when he wrote an account of his time in the service of Gordon, he did little more than pen a smear of the man.[11]

Despite the ongoing hardships of the campaign and Gordon's difficulties with personnel some positive results emerged. The construction of the fortified stations was powerfully symbolic of Gordon's resolve to interdict the slave trade. "The natives see that the line of posts is a *fait accompli*— that we mean staying," he reported home. Meanwhile, partly because he wanted him out of his immediate purview and partly because thus far he was one of the few men who had maintained his health, Gordon had sent Chaille-Long as an emissary to Mtesa, the Bugandan king. His son and heir, Mwanga, would gain infamy in Britain in ten years time for martyring a Church of England missionary along with forty-five of his own people. These young Bugandan men had chosen to maintain their conversion to Christianity rather than to submit to Mwanga's authority, which included engaging in homosexual acts with him.[12] In 1875, Mtesa was happy enough, if a bit suspicious, to be approached by Gordon. Owing to his proximity to the Great Lakes, Mtesa was at the center of what he knew increasingly to be European aspirations in Central Africa, and he acted accordingly. Gordon had tried to entice his cooperation by offering to formalize Buganda's status as an independent kingdom under Egyptian suzerainty. Mtesa rejected the offer that Chaille-Long relayed, but not before an important geographic discovery was made. Ever since the time of Speke and Grant's expedition of a decade earlier, it was speculated that a large body of water existed between Lake Victoria and Lake Albert and that the Nile linked all three of them. Chaille-Long confirmed this hunch to be correct. He found the lake and named it Ibrahim after the khedive's father. It would later be renamed Lake Kyoga, but there was still no sure way of knowing if the Nile was navigable from Lado to Lake Victoria. If so, then Central Africa could be opened up to trade from within, and northern control of the route assured.

By 1876 the major task remaining in the region was to determine the course of the Nile as it approached the Great Lakes. Two years into his Sudanese assignment had led Gordon to a sustained relationship with the Kingdom of Buganda. It also meant a similar relationship with the nearby Kingdom of Bunyoro. The only way to ensure Egyptian control of both kingdoms was to determine the possibility of transporting boats by river and overland to Lake Victoria. If it was possible, then the massive lake could be patrolled and Egyptian suzerainty enforced. Earlier, in October 1875, Gordon dispatched Romolo Gessi with a force of one thousand men to conduct the circumnavigation of Lake Albert making him the first European to do so. While there, Gessi also came into contact with Kabarega, king of the Bunyoro. The presence of Gessi and his mostly Egyptian troops struck fear and panic in Kabarega, whose intimation that this reconnaissance could spell his eventual downfall was prescient. Gordon was pleased with Gessi's success: "The Lake is surveyed," he wrote to the Freeses in England, "and it is over. . . . No river enters it at south end."[13] The question remained of the link, if any, between Lakes Albert and Victoria. Did the Victoria Nile empty into Lake Albert? If so, did this mean that a navigable route between the two lakes was possible? As useful as Gessi's expedition had been, this pressing question had not yet been answered. Gordon therefore decided that he would try to answer it himself, and on July 20, 1876 he boarded the *Nyanza* to steam south from Dufile toward the lakes.

Gordon reached his initial destination, Lake Albert, in just longer than a week. The passage was fairly smooth and upon reaching Magungo, "a most miserable-looking place," the point where the Victoria Nile empties into the lake, he rested. The really tough slogging would now begin. For the next month or so Gordon and his small party ascended the Victoria

Nile as far as navigable, and then continued on foot. The Murchison Falls, so named in honor of the president of the Royal Geographical Society, were encountered within a few days. The chute is spectacular; the river plunges 130 feet through a gorge twenty feet wide. Of course, the falls meant the end of the steamer's usefulness. Clutching a small black notebook in which he entered his observations and calculations, Gordon began walking along the banks of the river. The forest cover was dense, the rains fell, and ravines serrated the land. "It is terrible walking . . . it is simply killing . . . I am nearly dead," recorded Gordon on a day when the temperature once again soared into the nineties.[14] He was determined to follow the Nile as far as Lake Kyoga despite the physical hardship.

As the tortuous expedition continued, Gordon received word that Mtesa was resisting khedivial overtures to come under Egyptian suzerainty. Earlier, Gordon had dispatched an officer and a detachment of men to demonstrate Egypt's intentions in Buganda by building a stockade. Gordon had specified a site at Ripon Falls (Urondogani), the place where the waters of Lake Victoria spill out to begin the Victoria Nile, to commence construction. The wily Mtesa had other ideas. He forced the stockade to be built at his capital of Rubega, and after construction was complete the 140 soldiers working on the project effectively became Mtesa's hostages. Further complicating matters was a newly established mission station—the forerunner of the station Mwanga would severely persecute ten years later—in Buganda whose support came from England and whose missionaries were not interested in falling under Egyptian control. Gordon tried to convince them otherwise, but ultimately they did not listen.

Once again, Gordon would have to try to negotiate an agreement with the Bugandan king, who earlier had assured Gordon that "I want to be a friend of the English." Gordon made a treaty offer at the end of August and selected his new medical officer to deliver it. Emin Pasha was an expatriate German physician who had converted to Islam and dropped his name of Edouard Schnitzer, which was why Gordon chose him to be the messenger. Emin proceeded to Rubega in September.[15] He met with Mtesa and his ministers; the king wore "a huge white turban, dressed in gold-embroidered clothes, holding in one hand a silver-mounted sword, and in the other a sort of carved sceptre."[16] At first, the meeting did not go well. Nothing was said by anyone for ten minutes. Mutual offenses of various kinds then ensued. Finally, however, an understanding was reached. The ill-fated Egyptian garrison would be allowed to leave unimpeded, but there would be no treaty and therefore no annexation. The khedive's plans to turn the Great Lakes region into an extension of Egypt would not take place. As for Gordon, he could see that his mission was nearly complete and he decided to head for home soon.

Before resigning, he carried on with the remainder of his Nile explorations. The balance of September was a continuation of the survey: slogging through the forest, swatting away all manner of insects, and, as he noted in the midst of composing a letter home, "I have killed a nasty viper in my tent this minute."[17] He was grateful, though, that not much killing, either of African natives or of Europeans, had taken place. The achievements of the expedition were considerable. Apart from the work of Chaille-Long and Gessi, Gordon himself had explored the Nile from Magungo to an area north of Lake Kyoga. The stations established along the river had effectively cut off the slave trade's southern reach into Equatoria. There was nothing, however, that Gordon could do about the invidious slave hunts in the provinces of Darfur, Kordofan, and the Bahr el Ghazal in which Egyptian and Sudanese government officials connived. The great slaver, Zubair Rahmat, who would soon enter Gordon's life in a decisive manner, ruled in those regions and his iniquitous commerce was beyond Gordon's control. Still, Equatoria itself was in considerably better shape than when he had first arrived in 1874. Gordon had not been successful in his quest to annex Buganda and Bunyoro for the khedive, but his exploratory work on Egypt's behalf would strengthen the khedive's claims to the region, should they be pursued later.

Having arrived in Lado a few days earlier, on October 16, Gordon left by steamer bound for Khartoum. He reached it two weeks later, stayed a short time, and then continued north to Cairo. He was exhausted and had a strong desire to experience some of the comforts of home, including lying "in bed till eleven every day . . . in fact, get into a dormant state, and stay there till I am obliged to work. I want oysters for lunch."[18]

Gordon's decision to resign was met with dismay by the khedive and a long and frank discussion at Cairo's Abdin Palace ensued. Finally, Gordon was convinced to rethink his decision and, after taking a rest, return to Equatoria. Having made no absolute promises about a potential return, however, Gordon left for London and arrived home on Christmas Eve. He had been out of England for almost three years, but the country had not forgotten him. A few days after returning home the *Times* ran an article praising his anti-slaving work in Central Africa. The next day the editor gave his opinion about the growing debate concerning the fate of Bulgaria's beleaguered Christians, who were suffering intense persecution and death under the oppressive Ottoman Empire. The editor advocated Gordon as the right person to be sent as an emissary of the European powers: "Surely his genius for government and command might be profitably utilized nearer home. If the jealousies of the Powers would permit him to be made Governor of Bulgaria, he would soon make that province peaceful as an English county."[19] Nothing came of it, nor of the concurrent possibility, proposed by some, of Gordon heading up an East Africa Company modeled along the lines of the storied, though dissolved, East India Company.

Gordon himself continued to be unsure of whether or not to return to the Sudan. He sought the advice of the foreign secretary, Lord Derby, on January 11, 1877, the result of which was an apparent decision not to go. After mulling over the point for a few days, he telegraphed the khedive to tell him that he would not be returning. Two days later, a return cable arrived from Cairo reminding Gordon of what the khedive took to be a commitment to return made at their meeting in December. Appealing to Gordon's honor in this regard, he concluded by writing: "I shall expect you back according to your promise."[20] The khedive's appeal hit its mark and Gordon decided that, even if no promise had been made, he would go back to North Africa. A few friends in London, including Gerald Graham, suggested that in exchange for going he should demand of the khedive the governor generalship of the entire Sudan, not simply a reprise of control over Equatoria. Gordon agreed and said that he would make his intentions clear to Ismail in person. On January 31, five weeks after returning to England, he left again for Cairo.

Gordon reached the Egyptian capital on February 8. A few days later he met with the khedive. The meeting was momentous, because at the end of it, Gordon wrote, "he gave me the Soudan."[21] As desired, the khedive made him governor general. He became viceroy of one million square miles of territory and was charged with eradicating the slave trade and improving communications. Unknown to Gordon, back in London Gerald Graham had seen Lord Derby to press the case for his friend's appointment as governor general. Derby had been convinced by Graham and others and had instructed the British consul general in Cairo, Hussey Vivian, to speak directly to the khedive. Fairly bursting with pride, Graham wrote Gordon to tell him about his interview with Derby. Noting that having done so would likely result in his being seen as a "meddlesome ass," he did not care as long as it might help to "keep you out of those beastly African swamps."[22] Indeed, it did help, and Gordon never again set foot in Equatoria. By the time Graham's lighthearted letter reached Gordon, he was already en route to deal with his first crisis elsewhere, in Abyssinia.

Egypt and Abyssinia were in dispute over a territory called Senheit by the former and Bogos by the latter. The year before, while Gordon was in Equatoria, an Egyptian army had been defeated there by King Johannes (John), the Abyssinian ruler. The khedive was anxious to reach a treaty with King John and Gordon was to be his diplomatic instrument. This mission was Gordon's first as governor general, and it introduced him to a signature feature of life in the desert: long-range camel riding. Setting out from the Red Sea coast on his "immense command," Gordon rode south toward Abyssinia and an expected interview with King John.[23] Camels are notoriously difficult beasts to ride, and Gordon's initial experience with them proved the point. "Nearly everything is broken;" he wrote to Augusta, "pelting along on the camels ought eventually to shake one's organs out of their places." He quickly mastered the "perverse" ship of the desert and grew to love speeding across the sand over distances of up to forty-five miles a day.[24]

Near the end of March, Gordon reached Keren, the capital of the disputed Senheit/Bogos territory. King John, however, was not there, having gone on campaign elsewhere against a rival to his throne. Gordon decided, rather than wait around for the unpredictable king, he would continue to survey his new fiefdom and headed southwest toward the Blue Nile, which then took him to Khartoum. He arrived by boat on May 4 and the city was awaiting his entrance with great anticipation. "Missionaries and merchants, priests and Ulemas," the *Times* would later report, "all crowded to see him. But it is above all the poor country people who look upon him as their saviour."[25] The next day he was installed as governor general in the town square; the brief ceremony was looked upon by a cheering local population, including many slaves. Gordon kept his first public words in the Sudanese capital short and, for a former surveyor, apt: "With the help of God I will hold the balance level."[26] He then retired to the governor's palace, the *saraya*, located on the banks of the Blue Nile at the center of town and got down to business.

"I have been four days here, and have got through a great deal of work," he soon recorded in his top floor study, which gave him a view up and down the river.[27] Much of that work had to do with instituting various bureaucratic changes. One change that had an immediate and favorable effect was ending the punishment of public flogging in the town square, a practice that the old regime had meted out with the hated *courbash* whip to ten or fifteen people a day. Gordon also made himself available to the townspeople by erecting at the door of the palace "a box with a slit in the lid for petitions . . . and every one can put his petition in it." Another greatly popular change instituted by Gordon was the disbanding of the hated Turkish militia, the *Bashi-Bazouks*, a six-thousand-man force of thugs used by the former regime to inflict pain, suffering, and arbitrary "justice" on the population. Gordon moved quickly in this regard and concluded that the "people like me." He remained unmoved by the argument that Constantinople had made, one that Cairo would later use in 1884, that the local Muslim population would not stand for a Christian governor. Gordon found out otherwise, commenting straightforwardly: "the people want justice."[28]

The unresolved Abyssinian issue festered in the north, but Gordon's concerns lay mostly with moving quickly and decisively against the slave trade. To that end he planned a tour of the heartland of the trade, the western districts of Darfur and Kordofan. He set out on May 19, and planned to be away from Khartoum for the next four months. "I need the physical exertion," he explained in a letter home, "and am not afraid of these vast deserts. I have thirty camels." And so off he went, relieving garrisons, firing corrupt administrators, and slowly bringing relative peace to the turbulent backcountry. Gordon's remarked that his great desire was "to be a shelter to the people, to ease their burdens, and to soften their hard lot in these inhospitable lands."[29] Though there were those in England among the abolitionist community who thought doing so was rather easy, Gordon knew that ending the slave trade and slavery by fiat was impossible. Gradualism was the answer and he informed Hussey Vivian in Cairo of a plan on which he had been working that would require all slaves to be registered by January 1, 1878. After that date, any unregistered slave would be legally free. The institution itself would be prohibited incrementally throughout both Egypt and Sudan, Gordon proposed, with complete abolition coming in 1889. Vivian was impressed with Gordon's scheme and quickly ensured that it became the basis for the Anglo-Egyptian Convention for the Suppression of the Slave Trade signed in August 1877.

In the meantime, Gordon continued his visits, a European swooping into view on one of his camels in a way that "quite astonishes the Arabs," he wrote.[30] Perhaps the most astonished Arab to encounter Gordon in this period was a young slave trader named Suleiman Rahmat, whose lofty position in the trade was guaranteed by his powerful father, Zubair. In early September, they met at Dara, a dusty slavers' den in the middle of Darfur. Their meeting would prove to be perhaps the most dramatic encounter of Gordon's life.

The region was in an uproar. In 1874, Zubair had invaded Darfur intent on winning it for Egypt and being rewarded by the khedive for adding it to his Sudanese territories. Ismail feared Zubair's growing power, however, and after detaining him at Cairo, the khedive sent Zubair to head up an Egyptian contingent fighting with Turkey against the Russians in the latest flare-up of the eastern question in the spring of 1877. Meanwhile, the imposition of harsh Egyptian control on Darfur caused enormous resentment among the downtrodden slaves. Much of their animus was stoked by the slavers' intention of winning Darfur for themselves. Suleiman, one of these local slave chieftains, was in the vanguard of this turmoil. By the summer of 1877, he had allied himself to others of a similar mind, and Darfur seethed with unrest and violence. Having left Khartoum in May, Gordon rode into the slavers' cauldron, intent on putting down Suleiman and his colleagues and reasserting Egyptian suzerainty in the outlaw province. Doing so, he believed, would lead ultimately to the abolition of the slave trade in Darfur.

On the morning of September 2 at Dara, Gordon rose at daybreak as usual and dressed. Instead of putting on his normal khaki attire he donned the governor general's uniform of gold brocade given to him by the khedive.

The garment was spectacular and designed to induce respect, even awe. Suleiman was camped nearby and Gordon, never without a sense of irony, selected "an escort of *my* robbers . . . rode out to the camp of the other robbers about three miles off." The scene he encountered there was menacing. Suleiman commanded a band of three thousand men and boys, well armed, "fierce, unsparing, the terror of Central Africa," as Gordon put it. At just twenty-two years of age, Suleiman was little more than a boy himself, but he commanded the respect and allegiance of his slavers' army.

Resplendent in his uniform, the sun glinting off the gold brocade, Gordon rode through their brooding midst up to Suleiman's tent. Accepting a traditional glass of water, Gordon then instructed Suleiman to return to Dara, which he did. Once there, Gordon gave Suleiman and his advisers, "in choice Arabic" and in "a pantomime of signs," a reprise of their heinous crimes. Gordon concluded his harangue with the ultimatum that if they did not stop ravaging the country and cease their open revolt against the khedive's authority then he would have no choice but to "disarm them and break them up." Linguistically, Gordon was no Richard Burton, the great explorer of Africa who was fluent in at least twenty-one languages, and therefore it is not surprising that his dressing down of Suleiman and his men accompanied by wild gesticulations left them "stupefied." Gordon, well aware that the whole scene was "quite absurd," nonetheless waited for Suleiman's response. The young slaver and his supporters had arrived at Gordon's encampment "armed to the teeth," a discourtesy in the desert, and if Suleiman chose to fight it was very likely that victory would have been his.[31] Looking "daggers" at him, Suleiman retired to ruminate on his unappealing choice. "Poor little chap!" a tense Gordon recorded during the next three days while he waited for an answer, "he has a bitter time of it before him, and before he realises the nothingness of the world; brought up in the midst of the most obsequious people and slaves, accustomed to do just what he liked, to think nothing of killing people, or of their misery, and now to be *nothing!*"

Finally, on September 5, the tension broke; Suleiman sent word to Gordon that he was departing for his base at Shaka. The possibility of a fight remained, however, as a fierce debate was taking place between Suleiman and his fellow slavers' about whether or not to resist Gordon. It gradually dissipated, and Suleiman asked Gordon for the governorship of

Bahr el-Ghazal as a consolation. Gordon refused the request, stunned by its impertinence, especially as the "cub" was unwilling to pledge allegiance to the khedive. He did give Suleiman a vice governorship of the region eventually, in an attempt to ensure his support, but Gordon never trusted him. The Darfur revolt had been avoided, but Suleiman was angry and not fully placated. He would be heard from again.[32]

As much as Gordon's success in putting down the revolt in Darfur and in making serious inroads against the slave trade pleased the khedive, he had bigger problems closer to home. His regime was a financial shambles, fully half its annual income paying interest to European bondholders who held Egypt's growing debt. The Europeans established a debt commission, whose remit was to examine Egyptian finances and, against the khedive's objection, determine the nature of the regime's expenditures. Gordon was taken away from his preferred task of traversing his desert kingdom to break up the slave trade and improve Sudan's communications infrastructure, and was called to Cairo to assist the khedive. He left Khartoum in early February 1878 and steamed north.

By the time Gordon reached Cairo a month later, the khedive was frantic about his weakening position. Interest payments on the debt meant that civil and military wages were far in arrears. The Russo-Turkish War demanded Egyptian money and men, and English and French bondholders were castigating the khedive for what they said was personal profligacy. English interest in Egyptian finances had begun to increase in 1875 when the Disraeli government purchased the khedive's 45 percent share in the Suez Canal Company. In 1876, Egyptian government debt was estimated at a staggering eighty-one million pounds, most of it carried by European investors. The agricultural peasant society of Egypt, the *fellahin,* which composed the country's tax base, simply could not support the 7 percent interest rate charged on the debt, and the outcome was a severe financial crisis. The answer, as far as Britain and France were concerned, was a full-scale inquiry into Egyptian finances; the result of which the khedive rightly suspected would be his deposition. Gordon, newly arrived on the scene, and staying at Ismail's magnificent Abdin Palace, had a different plan: suspend interest payments for a year to pay at least the wages of the clerks and the soldiers. In a later age, such a suggestion might have been lauded as

Gordon by Adams & Scanlan

A final photograph. A pensive Gordon on the eve of his last
departure for the Sudan, 1884.

Baker by Whitlock

Sir Samuel Baker, Gordon's predecessor in the Sudan during the 1870s and an irrepressible Victorian globe-trotter, c. 1870.

Gordon by Clifford

Gordon in Victorian profile, complete with mutton-chop whiskers and signature moustache, 1882.

Rockstone Place by Faught

No. 5 Rockstone Place, Southampton, as it looks today.
Gordon's refuge in England.

Gladstone by Elliott & Fry

W. E. Gladstone at the
beginning of his second
administration, display-
ing the stern visage
characteristic
of his frosty view of
Gordon, 1880.

Gordon by Pellegrini

Gordon caricatured
as part of the series,
Men of the Day,
in *Vanity Fair*, 1881.

Leopold II by Bassano

Leopold II, King of the
Belgians, almost
Gordon's patron,
who planned to employ
him in the Congo once
he had returned from
Khartoum, 1889.

Queen Victoria by Bassano

Queen Victoria, Gordon's champion, celebrating the golden anniversary of her reign, two years after the fall of Khartoum,1887.

Wolseley by Bassano

Garnet, Lord Wolseley, the quintessential Victorian general, sent unsuccessfully to relieve Gordon at Khartoum, c. 1880.

Gordon by Faught

The Gordon Memorial bronze statue by Hamo Thornycroft. First erected in St. Martin's Place in 1888 and then moved to Trafalgar Square, it is located today along the Victoria Embankment.

Gordon by Joy

As Victorians saw him: "General Gordon's Last Stand," by George William Joy, 1887.

The Taiping Campaign, 1860–64, *by Andrew Gregg*

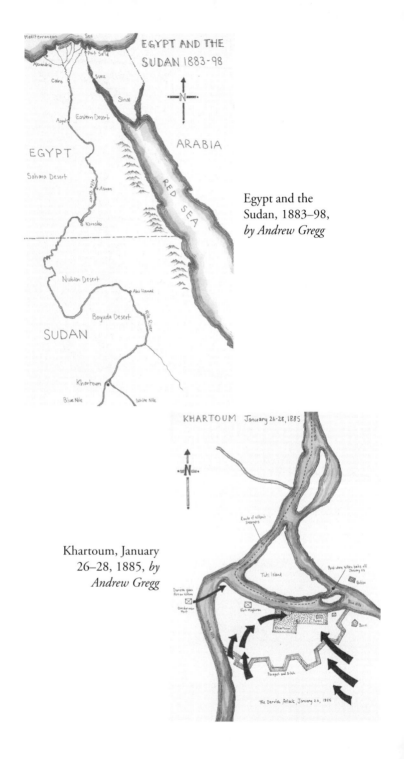

Egypt and the
Sudan, 1883–98,
by Andrew Gregg

Khartoum, January
26–28, 1885, *by
Andrew Gregg*

farsighted and humane. Not so in 1878. The head of the English commissioners, Evelyn Baring—later ennobled as Lord Cromer to play a critical part in the history of late nineteenth- and early twentieth-century Egypt—thought the idea and its sponsor ridiculous. "Altogether," wrote Baring, "he impresses me so far as an excellent, simple-hearted, and impracticable man about as much fit for the work he has in hand as I am to be Pope."[33]

For his part, Gordon was not ignorant of the complexities of what lay behind Egyptian finances and the bondholders' demands. His own experience in Sudan was replete with attempts to raise revenue and balance budgets. He had little time for Baring, whom he found to have "a pretentious, grand, patronizing way about him. We had a few words together . . . When oil mixes with water, we will mix together."[34] Gordon's first impressions of Baring did not change much over time, and were in accord with those of many others who collectively gave him a nickname that stuck: "Over-Baring." In any event, Gordon was given no official standing at the Cairo inquiry, even though the khedive wished him to chair it, and he left in March 1878. As for the khedive, he fought to retain control but his rule had only a short time to continue. In June 1879 he abdicated in favor of his son, Tewfik, although he was actually forced out mainly by Britain and France. Egyptian finances continued to suffer until they combined with nationalism to engender a revolt in 1882. In the meantime, a disgusted and disillusioned Gordon who felt "any efforts I recommended [were] useless," as he wrote to Gerald Graham, was pleased to leave Cairo and return to Khartoum in June.[35]

For the next nine months until March of 1879, Gordon never left the capital. His time was spent primarily completing administrative work that came to bore him intensely, especially by comparison to his desert passages and brushes with danger in the camp of Suleiman. Nevertheless, he knew it was necessary to ensure that Sudan was solvent, especially in light of what was happening to the khedive. He convinced both Cairo and London that Sudan should be seen as financially sovereign. A substantial deficit existed, which he set out to eradicate by economizing where he could, including limiting Sudan's far-reaching administration to north of Lake Victoria. Also, he canceled a southern extension of the railway along the Nile from Wadi Halfa. "I have been very hard at work with the accounts," he wrote home, "and have done a good business."

Owing to an unusually high river, Sudan saw malaria outbreaks reach epidemic levels in the fall and winter of 1878. Mosquitoes by the millions buzzed through the air. Sickness was rampant, and even the usually resistant Gordon succumbed, as he reported to Augusta: "I was so seedy two or three days ago, in my vast lonely house, quite alone."[36] By February 1879, however, he had reason to perk up. He had received a report of rebellion in the Bahr el Ghazal. The rebellion was led by the disaffected Suleiman (whom Gordon had named the southern province's vice governor in the fall of 1878) and was similar to the one he raised in Darfur almost two years earlier. Gordon was determined to stamp out this new threat as he had the original one.

Earlier, in July 1878, Gordon had sent Romolo Gessi to Bahr el Ghazal in an attempt to control and eventually end the slaving power of Suleiman. Over the next six months, Gessi had engaged in a number of fierce battles with the youthful vice governor and rebel. Early in 1879 Suleiman had been considerably weakened by Gessi's relentless pursuit and had appealed far and wide for reinforcements from the slavers of Bahr el Ghazal. They took up the cause, in large part because of their hatred of Gordon and his abolitionism, and likeminded slavers from Darfur and Kordofan—still smarting from Gordon's success in cowing Suleiman there—also joined. Departing Khartoum in mid-March, Gordon's plan was to enlarge his troop strength as he went along by picking up willing soldiers, and then, working in combination with Gessi, "deal a death-blow to the slave trade."[37]

Unbeknownst to Gordon, around the same time he was marching out of Khartoum en route for Suleiman's headquarters at Shaka, which he branded the "wretched place," and "a nest of slavers," Gessi was hot on the trail of the young rebel.[38] He had tracked him to his distant redoubt, the remote and strongly fortified town of Dem Suleiman in southwestern Bahr el Ghazal, and was able to capture the town's critical water source. He then attacked. Victory came easily because without water and under heavy bombardment almost all of Suleiman's men fled, as he did himself. Gessi pursued him north into Darfur. Gordon, traveling south and west from Khartoum, was closing in on Suleiman, too. At the end of June Gordon and Gessi met near Shaka, at the desolate village of Taweisha, to determine their final strategy. "We talked for some hours," wrote Gessi later, " . . . employed in discussing the means and mode of capturing Suleiman, who still held the field with a nucleus of followers, and was still able to carry desolation into the countries he traversed."[39]

The two men decided that Gessi would carry on until Suleiman was apprehended or killed, and that Gordon, once settling the scraggly band of 450 slaves he had freed while on campaign, would return to Khartoum. Gessi set out after Suleiman and caught him within a month. In his haste to escape his pursuers the young slaver had divided his three thousand troops into three groups, and then with a smaller escort of chosen men, had hived off further still. Nevertheless, Gessi tracked him relentlessly while maintaining a high degree of invisibility and approached Suleiman's encampment on July 14. The next day as dawn broke, Gessi sent a message to the surprised and quickly enraged Suleiman: "I give you five minutes to surrender. That time passed, I shall attack you from all sides. Remember that you are surrounded."[40] Gessi had only 250 men with him but his small band of fighters proved to be enough. Panic in the trapped camp ensued. Realizing his hopeless position, Suleiman and his henchmen duly surrendered. Gordon had authorized Gessi to kill the captured rebel, but Gessi waited to see evidence of his plan to escape before executing Suleiman on July 15.

The execution of Suleiman had important ramifications for Gordon. The slave trade in southern Sudan had been essentially broken up. News of Gessi's success reached Gordon in Khartoum on July 21. He was pleased, but the news also confirmed that his time in Sudan should be brought to an end. Exhausted by more than five years in the desert, he had again decided to resign. "I am a wreck," he wrote that day, "like the portion of the 'Victory' towed into Gibraltar after Trafalgar; but God has enabled me, or rather has used me, to do what I wished to do—that is, break down the slave-trade."

Contributing to his decision (one first intimated to Cairo in March) was the fact that the khedive had just been deposed from office by the Ottoman sultan, who had acted under intense pressure from the European powers. Gordon was informed of this "great international injustice" while still on campaign in Darfur. "May worse come to those who have wrought this," wrote a sympathetic friend to Gordon from the Ministry of Finance in Cairo.[41] Having decided to resign, Gordon wasted no time in departing Khartoum. A week later he boarded a steamer bound for Cairo, and arrived near the end of August. Before shipping out for England he had one piece of important unfinished business concerning King John of Abyssinia. The dispute over territory between Egypt and Abyssinia that Gordon addressed in 1874 had not been resolved in the intervening years. It seemed that King John was now willing to sign a peace treaty, so Gordon set off on the last day of August to obtain the monarch's signature to put the festering issue to rest.

Weary, but as usual determined to succeed, it took Gordon almost six weeks of riding a mule "wending my way over the worst of roads and steepest of mountains" to reach King John's remote capital of Debra Tabor.[42] The point of the diplomatic exercise now seemed moot to Gordon, however, since he had learned while steaming south through the Red Sea that the disputed province of Senheit/Bogos was now permanently occupied by the Abyssinians and therefore beyond the reach of conventional diplomacy. If Egypt was serious about reclaiming the territory, it would likely mean war: "it is not a question of ceding or not ceding the country, but of retaking it," wrote Gordon[43] If not for the real grief and brutality meted out by the king to his helpless people (cutting off noses, lips, hands, and feet, putting out eyes), Gordon's exercise in mountain-top diplomacy might have seemed comic. King John, who "calls himself the 'God-given Ruler,'" finally received Gordon, showing only his eyes while perched on a raised dais. "Cows, mules, & ass," he recorded, "allowed entry into His Majesty's presence." [44] Having not read the letters sent to him by the khedive, the king called for them to be brought in and translated, as well as for the hapless clerk who apparently had not furnished them earlier. The poor courtier then received "forty blows," according to Gordon.[45] As for the king, once having read the letters—essentially a list of disputed points over which negotiations could commence—Gordon asked him if he would write out his list of demands for the Egyptian government. "Yes," replied John, followed immediately by, "I am going to take some hot baths two days from here; come with me."[46]

The negotiations were a farce and resolved nothing. Gordon was not, however, allowed by the king to leave until late November. On December 8, Gordon finally reached Massawa on the Red Sea coast and exactly one month later, on January 8, 1880, after reporting his findings to an unhappy Khedive Tewfik in Cairo, Gordon boarded ship in Alexandria for the first leg of his journey back to England. Before sailing, he gave an interview to a correspondent from the *Times*. Summing up his accomplishments in Sudan, a tired but not despairing Gordon said, "I am neither a Napoleon nor a Colbert; I do not profess to have been either a great ruler or a great financier; but I can say this—I have cut off the slave dealers in their strongholds and I have made all my people love me."[47] He passed his forty-seventh birthday en route home and by February was reclining in Augusta's parlor in Southampton.

A Roving Commission

Gordon arrived in Southampton in February 1880 rested after touring Italy briefly but still exceedingly tired from his arduous service in Sudan. As a result, he decided that he needed a thorough rest and that a lake in Switzerland was the only place to get it. For the next couple of months he relaxed in Lausanne, Berne, and elsewhere in the crisp air and bright sunshine of the Alps. During this self-imposed idyll, Gordon put his immediate future on hold, even though his services were keenly sought after by various parties including the British government and the Belgian King Leopold II, whose colonial misadventure in the Congo was beginning its great rush forward following H. M. Stanley's celebrated recent peregrinations there.[1] After returning to London in April, Gordon occupied himself with settling into semi permanent lodgings at 114 Beaufort Street, a row house in Chelsea located near his brother Henry, and by meeting with various people such as the saintly Florence Nightingale and the steely Isabel Burton. Burton encouraged him to use his presumed influence at the foreign office to secure a diplomatic post for her out-of-favor husband Richard. Gordon did as he was asked, but his efforts on behalf of the brilliant but iconoclastic linguist and explorer fell on deaf ears.

"I have written letters to the F.O. that would raise a corpse;" he explained to her, "it is no good."[2]

Gordon's own uncertain future was settled with the fall of the Disraeli government in April. The election that followed saw Gladstone's liberals return to office, and among the new government's many appointments was the Marquis of Ripon as Viceroy of India. After Disraeli's "forward" policy in India, which included initiating the Second Afghan War in an attempt to thwart Russian ambitions in the region, Gladstone planned a reforming administration there, with the progressive-minded Ripon in the vanguard. After accepting the viceroyalty Ripon asked Gordon to be his private secretary. It is unclear why Ripon thought Gordon would be the man to give him signal assistance. Perhaps Gordon's reputation as a champion of native rights influenced Ripon. Certainly the press coverage of the appointment was favorable, if a bit puzzled by it: "There is something whimsical in turning Gordon Pasha—Chinese Gordon—into a Private secretary and sending him to Simla," wrote the *Daily News*.[3] Ripon's five years in India did bring reform, as well as unrest, particularly in the controversy over what came to be called the Ilbert Bill, legislation designed to give Indians a large measure of equality with Europeans before the law in the bellwether state of Bengal.[4] Gordon played no part in the reform or the unrest, because he began to have severe reservations about going to India with Ripon. The job was an important one but not one for which the career soldier and former governor general was suited temperamentally.

The vice-regal party duly departed for Bombay in mid-May, Gordon among them, but within a few days he had come to the irrevocable conclusion that he had made a mistake. "Lord Ripon very kind [sic]," he reported to Augusta during a brief stopover in Aden, "but I cannot say I like the berth, and I shall get away as soon as I can do so in a respectable manner." A few days later he wrote her to say that he had decided "to leave either in September or the beginning of October." But, as it turned out, even these proximate dates were not soon enough. Two days after arriving in Bombay he resigned. "India is the most wretched of countries," he wrote by way of explanation. "The way Europeans live there is absurd in its luxury. . . . How truly glad I am to have broken with the whole lot. . . . All this private secretaryship and its consequent expenses are due to my not acting on my *own* instinct. However, for the future I will be wiser." He explained to his brother Henry that he blamed a "moment of weakness" for having accepted the appointment in the first place. In any event, it was done: he had peremptorily resigned.[5]

The mercurial Gordon was evidenced, but Ripon did not seem to mind. "We parted the best of friends . . .," the viceroy wrote to a colleague, "my respect for him has in many ways increased rather than diminished."[6] Consequently, Gordon and Ripon remained on good terms and corresponded occasionally, as in the summer of 1881 when the viceroy reported that his "first year of office has been a very anxious one [it included the retaking of Afghanistan, lost in 1878]."[7] He was keen to know what Gordon, at that point in the Cape Colony in South Africa, was doing. The last time Ripon had seen him Gordon was about to depart for Hong Kong. He would be going back to China, if only briefly, because the day after he resigned from Ripon's service, he was asked by telegram to leave immediately for his former Oriental haunt. He agreed and did so right away, booking passage on a cargo ship—"It is twenty years ago since I came out to China"—and steamed into port on July 3, 1880.[8]

The timing of the invitation to return to China was remarkably fortuitous. Indeed, it was so timely that Gordon was conscious of his potential for looking bad in the eyes of those who might suspect him of leaving the nascent viceroy in the lurch. To this end, he instructed Augusta to "let it be known that I resigned before I knew of the China telegram, for otherwise it would seem that I had left Lord Ripon for this affair, which is not the case; when I resigned, I knew nothing of what I should do."[9] "This affair," as Gordon termed it, was an invitation from China's inspector general of customs, Sir Robert Hart, to help reorganize and make battle-ready the Imperial Chinese Army, which was expecting a clash with Russia. The two countries were in a dispute over the Chinese province of Sinkiang. Located in the remote, far northwest corner of the country, it abutted the Russian-controlled territory of Turkistan. Tsar Alexander II, in what became the last year of his rule, was directing his country in the throes of eastward expansion and did not wish to be fenced in by China, whose sovereignty over Sinkiang he did not accept. The dispute that began as a diplomatic contest threatened to boil over into war.

Gordon's precipitate acceptance of Hart's offer caused an immediate uproar at the war office in London, which feared a reprise of the semi-freelance Ever Victorious Army, only this time hopelessly arrayed against the might of imperial Russia. Telegrams flew back and forth. Gordon resigned from the British army, rather than "desert China in her present crisis."[10] He requested leave, which he wanted to use in service to China. The government remained firm against the idea, especially the British minister in Peking, Sir Thomas Wade. He ordered Gordon to go directly to the British legation in Hong Kong and remain there until further notice. Gordon, characteristically, ignored the order. He thought Wade was overreacting because, as Gordon had stressed on a number of occasions, he was not in China to initiate war: "My fixed desire is to persuade the Chinese not to go to war with Russia."[11] In August, when it came time for Gordon to give his views formally to the Chinese government—which British officials allowed him to do—he told them that making peace with the Russians was their only viable course of action. Some of the Chinese mandarins whom he addressed did not like the advice; they saw war with Russia as more honorable and potentially winnable. When Gordon left for England after visiting old friends and touring sites connected with the EVA and the Taiping Rebellion, he pessimistically believed a war would break out in the near future. It did not. Early in 1881, China and Russia signed the Treaty of St. Petersburg, in which Gordon's recommendations were included. By that time, however, he was long gone.

After reaching England in October, Gordon—at loose ends again and officially on six-months' leave—decided to go to Ireland. The visit was a spur-of-the-moment, private economic and social fact-finding mission, prodded by the serial miseries of the place and owing to the fact that Gladstone had made it his government's chief mission to fix what ailed Ireland or, to use the prime minister's term from years earlier, to "pacify" it.[12] Gordon spent a little more than two weeks there, landing at Cork, and making his way through green farm country to the south and west. The grinding poverty of the Irish peasantry appalled him, set off as it was by the grandeur of their Anglo-Irish landlords' Georgian mansions. The chief political and economic question was ownership and tenancy of the land, a point just then being made more forcefully than ever by Charles Stewart Parnell and the Land League.

Gordon saw enough injustice in his two weeks in Ireland to quickly pen a polemical, six-page memorandum, which he sent to Gladstone. In sometimes florid language, similar to that used by the prime minister himself when speaking of the tribulations suffered by the Bulgarians under Ottoman rule a few years earlier, Gordon sounded forth about the plight of the downtrodden Irish. "The peasantry of the Northwest and Southwest of Ireland," charged Gordon, "are much worse off than any of the inhabitants of Bulgaria, Asia Minor, China, India or the Sudan." Having been to all of the places named, he was speaking with the voice of authority, but Gladstone did not appreciate Gordon's intervention in the highly contentious Irish question. The "scandal" that was Ireland's condition could only be made right by profoundly altering the relationship between landlord and people, contended Gordon. The way to do that, he suggested, was to take a page out of the British government's method of ending slavery within the empire in the 1830s. That is, the great Anglo-Irish landlords needed to be bought out by the government, in the same way that the Caribbean plantation owners (of which Gladstone's father was one) had been paid off to the tune of £20 million. This way the Irish people would be given justice and at a stroke the specter of interminable political protest would end, as "they would have nothing more to seek from agitation."[13]

Gordon's brief intervention in Ireland's affairs was never repeated, although one could argue that some of his ideas would later appear in the British government's reforming land policy there. In any event, he had said his piece and spent the rest of the year visiting friends in the country to "disentangle myself from the world," as he wrote to Augusta.[14] By New Year 1881, he was living in London, meeting up again with Florence Nightingale, as well as with Alfred Lord Tennyson, whose poetry he admired and who would later memorialize Gordon. Both Nightingale and Tennyson were interested in Gordon's ideas on military reform, especially his suggestion that a method of army training for poor boys be established. (Ultimately, this idea was taken up after his death in 1885 as the memorial Gordon Boys Home, which today, in a much-modernized form, functions as the coeducational Gordon's School in Surrey.)

Gordon's pleasant winter and spring in London—his appearance in February in the "Men of the Day" series in *Vanity Fair* confirming, not altogether with his approval, certain fame—left him in the familiar position, however, of not knowing what might come next in his life. This brief period of uncertainty came to an end at the beginning of May when he was appointed Commander of the Royal Engineers on the faraway island of Mauritius. Once again, Charles Gordon would ship out hastily for an exotic location.

Located off the East African coast, Mauritius had come under British control during the Napoleonic Wars. A sugar-plantation island, following the abolition of slavery in the British Empire in 1833, Mauritius had almost half-a-million Indian indentured workers by Gordon's arrival in 1881.[15] He arrived at its tiny capital, Port Louis, in late June, charged with reporting on the state of the island's defenses, and those of its dependencies, which included the stunningly beautiful Seychelles archipelago to the north. Initially, Gordon was not keen about this assignment, which he considered a kind of tropical exile, but he soon began to work and explore. His explorations took him to the isolated island of Praslin in Seychelles, which Gordon concluded controversially was a very strong candidate for the biblical Garden of Eden.

He wrote and submitted a report of his findings to the Royal Commission on Empire Defense in August 1881. Titled, "Memorandum on Colonial Defenses," Gordon engaged in a wide-ranging discussion of Britain's strategic position in North Africa and the Indian Ocean rather than limiting his scope to Mauritius and its dependencies. In the memo, he dissented from the prevailing wisdom that the Suez Canal was important to the holding of India, and promoted the Cape Colony as the key route to the subcontinent. Arguing that the Suez Canal was one sunken ship away from being blocked, he advocated a strategic policy of less dependency on it. As for Mauritius itself, "this place is utterly without defence," he wrote not long after arriving. For the Royal Commission, his views did not change. Among his recommendations was splitting Mauritius and Seychelles into separate crown colonies and using them, with other important maritime locations, as vital links in a global chain of defense, and not as potential homes for settlers. Colonists in such places he regarded as a potential "nuisance," whose presence would inflame the resentments of the indigenous population and whose forbearance in matters of a strategic nature could not be counted on.[16]

As much as he came to enjoy it, Gordon's Mauritius command was brief, less than a year in duration. Early in April 1882, Gordon learned of his recent promotion to major general and was ordered to depart immediately for South Africa. He did so on April 4, enduring a "long weary passage" to Cape Town that left him "very seedy for some days. A sailing-vessel is indeed a trial," he opined to Augusta.[17] Gordon's destination, Cape Colony, was working out its constitutional relationship with Basutoland (today's Lesotho), a small, independent kingdom surrounded on all sides by the colony. The late king of Basutoland, Moshoeshoe, who ruled from a commanding mountaintop citadel, had intended to bring his people and territory under British protection to keep the expansionist Boers at bay.[18] The prospect of ruling additional African peoples was not one that either London or Cape Town necessarily welcomed. Meanwhile, the Sotho, the residents of Basutoland, were not united on the subject, and a rebellion had broken out led by one of Moshoeshoe's sons, Masupha, who refused to acknowledge the Cape's putative suzerainty over Basutoland. His half-brother, Letsie, however, was willing to work with the Cape.

Gordon's role in this delicate situation was unclear. He thought he might be made governor of Basutoland. Unfortunately, the acting governor's agent, Joseph Orpen, resented Gordon's arrival and saw him merely as an unofficial adviser. Accordingly, the two men did not get on well. Gordon finally made it to Basutoland in September, having first stopped en route to discuss the situation with Cecil Rhodes, at that time a decade into his great wealth and a member of the Cape's legislative assembly. The two men of empire each strongly impressed each other as independently minded, making it impossible to work side by side, but otherwise Rhodes remarked that they got on "capitally together."[19]

From his meeting with Rhodes, Gordon and a small party proceeded to Masupha's headquarters, Thaba Bosiu, the same mountaintop fortress occupied formerly by the great Moshoeshoe. Gordon made plain to the young rebel chieftain that if he failed to reach an agreement with the Cape, he would be at the mercy of the Boers, who were not interested in a negotiated settlement. But if he agreed then the Boers would be shut out and no harm would come to him from the British. Meanwhile, Masupha's rival in this affair, Letsie, decided to march his men on Thaba Bosiu and take it by force. Word of this impending attack reached Masupha and

Gordon at the same time. Gordon was surprised, Masupha outraged, assuming that he had been tricked. Gordon rightly protested his innocence, and blamed J. W. Sauer, the Cape's secretary of native affairs who had been negotiating with Letsie, for such saber rattling. Sauer himself, however, had been taken by surprise by Letsie's determination to attack and was chagrined at Gordon's potentially dangerous predicament. Gordon described it as "a completely false position" and chose to resign immediately, happy to be done with the Cape government, which he thought to be utterly incompetent. Still angry, he sailed for home in October. The issue was resolved rather quickly though, and along the lines Gordon had suggested. In December, Basutoland became autonomous from the Cape, and in 1884 while Gordon was in Khartoum, the British government decided to make it a protectorate. The Boers would never have it, and modern Lesotho would escape South African sovereignty and the tragic rigors of apartheid.

Once again, following his Basutoland assignment, Gordon was at loose ends. At sea, on the long voyage home from South Africa, he wrote to Augusta: "The King of the Belgians may ask me to go to the Congo. Query: Shall I go or not? . . . If I do not go there, then I shall go to Palestine."[20] Gordon chose Palestine.. After a brief visit home that saw him through Christmas he left for the Holy Land just before the New Year, arriving in Jerusalem on January 17, 1883.

Palestine in those days was a backwater province of the Ottoman Empire peopled by Arabs, a smattering of mostly Russian Jews, and various Christian pilgrims and missionaries from Europe and North America. Visiting the assorted sites connected with Christ's life and teaching was something Gordon had wished to do for some time, and he did so keenly, but his primary activity soon became trying to determine the exact location of Golgotha, the site of Christ's crucifixion and nearby resurrection. He came to believe these cardinal New Testament events were not associated with the Church of the Holy Sepulchre in the Old City of Jerusalem, a site over which the Roman Catholic and Orthodox Churches shared custody. Rather, Gordon argued that Skull Hill, located just outside the Old City near the Damascus Gate, was the actual Golgotha.

The idea of an alternative crucifixion site was not original to Gordon. The German archeologist, Otto Thenius, had proposed it first in the 1840s and it had gained some currency within professional and theological circles. Soon after Gordon's arrival in Jerusalem, he became convinced by Thenius's theory and began to draw maps and plot elevations, which, in his mind, confirmed the site as that written about in the Synoptic Gospels.[21] "I feel, for myself," he wrote to Augusta in January, "convinced that the hill near the Damascus Gate is Golgotha. From it you can see the Temple, the Mount of Olives, and the bulk of Jerusalem."[22] In the years after Gordon's brief residency in Jerusalem, his views were popularized within evangelical Protestantism especially, and "Gordon's Calvary," including the Garden Tomb located at the foot of Skull Hill, remains a place of pilgrimage for many.

Gordon's time in Palestine stretched into almost a full year. Apart from spending time at "*my* Golgotha," as he began to call it, he rode out into the Judean desert, struck up friendships with various missionaries and clerics, wrote copiously on the scriptures, and relocated to Jaffa on the Mediterranean coast to enlarge his explorations of the country.[23] During these months he had virtually nothing to do with the British army or government, although the French consul in Jerusalem assumed he was a spy and had him tailed.[24] That changed in mid-October when Gordon received a telegram sent on behalf of King Leopold, inviting him to serve in Africa. This overture, which Gordon readily accepted, eventually generated one of the most frantic and uncertain periods of his life. At the end of a three-month sojourn in London, Gordon left not for the Congo, as Leopold wished, but for Khartoum and what would be his ultimate assignment in the service of the British Empire.

Sudan II: Death in the Desert

After Gordon agreed to enlist in the service of King Leopold and resign his British army commission, he steamed out of Jaffa in mid-December. He boarded a train in Italy and pulled into Brussels on New Year's Day 1884. "I arrived here this morning at 8 a.m.," he wrote Augusta, "I am all right, in peace and tranquility."[1] The next day he met with the king who sported a long, full beard, which gave him the appearance of a patriarch of the Orthodox Church. Among other points of discussion, Leopold agreed to cover Gordon's forfeited army pension. Gordon then agreed to an early-February departure date for the Congo once he had formally resigned his commission in London and taken care of any other last bits of business. His task under Leopold would be to try to choke off the Central African slave trade; in the same way he had done successfully in southern Sudan. With that goal in mind, Gordon left Belgium for home, arriving at Rockstone Place in Southampton on January 7.

After arriving in Britain, Gordon began a hectic eleven days, during which his plans changed drastically at the hands of a conflicted British government that ultimately decided to return him to Sudan. During the previous year and a half, the Egyptian government, now essentially a client of Britain, had been under severe strain, battling a nationalist uprising led by a disaffected officer in its army, Col. Ahmad Arabi Pasha. The Egyptians were also endeavoring to cope with an even larger revolt in Sudan under the leadership of Mohammed Ahmed, who, styled as the Mahdi, had conquered much of the country and now threatened Khartoum. In Egypt, Arabi Pasha's revolt against the khedivial regime had been met with the Royal navy's successful bombardment of Alexandria in July 1882, followed in September with the complete destruction of Arabi's rebel forces at Tel el-Kebir and the country's occupation. In Sudan, however, a military mission under Col. William Hicks to find and rout the Mahdi and his men had resulted in disaster. In early November, while Gordon was completing his stay in Jaffa, Hicks was led deeper and deeper into the desert expanses of the province of Kordofan, and at Shaykan, his mostly Egyptian eight-thousand-man force was annihilated by Mahdi's forty thousand jihadists. Hicks' head was then cut off and taken to the Mahdi's camp at El Obeidwhere it was driven into a spike and raised high as a trophy of war. The defeat was total and the humiliation complete. As a result, both the British and Egyptian governments recognized that the best way forward was to evacuate Sudan's garrisons, along with any of the Egyptian and European population who wished to leave. Doing so would be immensely difficult, however, because with the victory at Shaykan the Mahdi's power over his people had become both mystical and overwhelming and he now exercised a close grip on the country, buttressed by the arms and ammunition taken from Hicks' defeated force.

Gordon's first intimation of the severity of the crisis in the Sudan, and his own role in solving it, had come just before he left Brussels for England. On January 4 he had received a letter from Garnet Wolseley, his old friend and colleague, who had led the highly successful attack on Arabi and his forces at Tel el-Kebir and was now adjutant general of the British army. General Wolseley knew of Gordon's recent agreement with King Leopold to go to the Congo and did not wish to see it carried out. Intimating that there might be something else Gordon could do instead, Wolseley wrote, "I hate the idea of your going to the Congo: You have had enough of liver-grilling climates . . . I wish I could have a long talk with you on Egyptian affairs, & hear your views on this Sudan question. The fact is the Egyptian gov't is totally incapable of ruling it."[2]

Wolseley was not the only one who wished to hear Gordon's views on Sudan. Around the war office, as Wolseley's words suggested, and elsewhere in the British government, Gordon's name was in the air. Gordon had long been a favorite of the press, too, and in light of the recent Hicks disaster they were more interested than ever in soliciting his opinions. Gordon had scarcely arrived at Rockstone Place on the evening of January 7 when Augusta gave him a telegram from the editor of the *Pall Mall Gazette*, the well-known W. T. Stead, requesting an interview to discuss the deteriorating situation in Sudan. Gordon declined, but rather than see the opportunity lost, Stead took the train down to Southampton the next morning, went the short distance from the station to Rockstone Place, and knocked on Augusta's front door. Though complaining of having been "invaded," a two-hour interview ensued as Gordon warmed gradually to the topic. He attributed the crisis in Sudan to a people in "despair." He rejected the idea that the Mahdi was an especially charismatic leader or that the movement was essentially religious in nature. Rather, to Gordon, Sudan's woes and its people's consequent uprising stemmed from their having been badly misgoverned. As Stead reported his words the next day in the *Gazette*, which was picked up immediately by the other London newspapers, Gordon contended that "during the three years that I wielded full powers in the Sudan, I taught the natives that they had a right to exist . . . I had taught them something of the meaning of liberty and justice, and accustomed them to a higher ideal of government than that which they had previously been acquainted." Gordon, like his Victorian contemporaries, had no experience with Islamic jihad as it would be witnessed in the next century, and so was quick and sincere in pointing solely at bad government as being the cause of the uprising. To some extent, Gordon was right in this assessment, and he saw diplomatic negotiation as the proper way to eventually bring about good government. "The Sudanese are very nice people," he told Stead. "They deserve the sincere compassion and sympathy of all civilized men. I got on very well with them."

Regarding diplomatic affairs in Egypt and Sudan involving Her Majesty's government, Gordon rejected the apparent decision to evacuate. "Even if we were bound to do so," he declaimed, "we should have said nothing about it. The moment it is known that we have given up the game, every man will go over to the Mahdi. All men worship the rising sun."[3]

Stead's reportage—"Chinese Gordon for the Sudan" he headlined his article—helped make Gordon the popular choice to solve the crisis. His reporting also was an important impetus in pushing the government to act, which it did barely longer than a week later. In the meantime, Gordon sought a bit of peace and quiet by visiting a couple of friends, including Sir Samuel Baker, now happily ensconced at his country house, Sandford Orleigh, in Devon. In comfortable retirement, the still-hearty Baker encouraged Gordon to return to Sudan.[4] A heightened but unsettled Gordon then returned to Southampton to find a telegram from Wolseley at the war office asking him to come to London to discuss the situation in Sudan. He agreed. What would be Gordon's final imperial appointment was now firmly in view.

After spending a "last quiet Sunday" with Augusta and taking care of final preparations (including writing his will) for his still-expected departure for the Congo, Gordon went to London on January 15 for his meeting with Wolseley.[5] Even though Gordon had formally resigned his commission on January 7, the government had not yet accepted it. The reason, explained Wolseley to a quizzical Gordon, was that the government had something else in mind for him to do in the near term, after which there would be no official objections to his proposed service under King Leopold and therefore he would be able to remain on the army's active list. Then Wolseley proceeded to the main reason for his interview with Gordon: "I asked him if he would go to Suakin to enquire into the condition of affairs in the Sudan. I told him he ought to go if the government asked him. He said he would go."[6]

The meeting continued as the two men discussed the deepening crisis in Sudan. Gordon, at Wolseley's request, wrote a list of proposed measures to be undertaken as part of the inquiry. The most basic of these measures describe Gordon's function to "report" on the military situation in Sudan, and then return home.[7] The meeting ended with the apparent understanding that Gordon would go to Sudan if Sir Evelyn Baring, British consul general in Cairo, agreed to the appointment. He then made a round of visits in London and set out for Brussels the next morning, still more sure of his service under Leopold than that possibly forthcoming with the British government. Gordon spent the evening of the sixteenth at his hotel in the Belgian capital. The next afternoon a telegram from Wolseley arrived asking him to return immediately to London. Gordon agreed, and after a hurried and uncomfortable meeting with King Leopold, at which Gordon told him that he must answer his country's call before enlisting in the service of another, he took the overnight boat train to London. He arrived the morning of January 18 and called on Wolseley at the war office, who told him that a meeting with certain members of the cabinet had been set for mid-afternoon.

Since Gordon's meeting with Wolseley three days earlier, a flurry of activity had been undertaken in London, and was about to result in the official decision to send Gordon back to Sudan. In Cairo Baring, who did not care for Gordon, initially had not wanted him or indeed any other British officer to be sent. However, owing to the increasingly unstable conditions in Sudan, he had changed his mind. He advised London that he "would rather have him [Gordon] than anyone else" and he made it clear that Gordon's role was to be both advisory and executive; that is, Baring was sure that the only option the Egyptian government now could exercise was to facilitate the evacuation of Sudan and Gordon was the man to do it. The job would be one of "great difficulty and danger," he warned, as there were twenty-one thousand Egyptian troops scattered throughout the country and eleven thousand civilians in Khartoum, all of whom wanted out.[8]

At Hawarden, his counter/estate Gladstone remained of the mind—based on a transcription of Gordon's original notes sent to him from Downing Street—that if Gordon were to go to Sudan it should be in a purely advisory capacity. As the prime minister put it: "In brief, if he reports what should be done, he should not be the judge *who* should do it, nor ought he to commit us on that point by advice officially given."[9] Gladstone's absence from London and his misunderstanding of the parameters of Gordon's mission as articulated later by the cabinet, would prove enormously influential in what transpired over the course of the next year.

On the afternoon of January 18, Gordon duly arrived at the war office to meet with a much-reduced cabinet. Only four ministers were in London and available for the meeting. The most important of them were Lord Granville, foreign secretary, and Lord Hartington, secretary of state for war. There is no detailed record of this momentous meeting and accounts vary as to precisely what was said during its brief duration, but the most thorough examination was undertaken by Bernard Allen.[10] His conclusion, based on Gordon's written and oral accounts of the meeting, statements made by the ministers present, and the official instructions issued by the government was that Gordon was charged with evacuating the Sudan. His job, therefore, was executive in nature, and not merely one of observation and reporting, which Gladstone, mistakenly, would always believe. As Gordon described the meeting in a letter to Augusta: "Wolseley came for me. I went with him and saw Granville, Hartington, Dilke and Northbrook; they said had I seen W. and did I understand their ideas. I said yes, and repeated what W. had said to me as to their ideas, which was '*they would evacuate Soudan.*' They were pleased and said, that was their idea. Would I go? I said 'yes.' They said 'when?' I said 'To-night.' And it was over."[11]

And so it was. A hurried departure ensued. A staff officer, Col. J. D. H. Stewart, was assigned to Gordon and final good-byes were made. At Charing Cross station, a short walk from the war office, a small party, including Granville and Wolseley, gathered on the platform. Gordon had no money with him so Wolseley rifled through his pockets for a few pounds and also handed him his gold watch.[12] Gordon and Stewart climbed aboard the 8 p.m. night-mail train and it began to chug south toward the English Channel. "I go to the Soudan to-night to finish a work," he wrote Augusta, "then to the Congo."[13] No one in England would ever see Charles Gordon again.

For Gordon, the weeklong passage to Egypt became a time of intense rumination. His first impressions of the crisis in Sudan made him think that evacuation was a mistaken policy. Yet, here he was charged, as far as he could tell, by the British government with doing just that. As he rumbled along in the train through France and then steamed across the Mediterranean in the SS *Tanjore* Gordon contemplated how best to complete his instructions from the cabinet. Back in London, the newspapers were exultant that their man was on his way to the crisis zone. "No step taken by Her Majesty's Government since the Egyptian troubles began," praised Stead's *Pall Mall Gazette*, "has ever evoked such a universal outburst of approval as the despatch of General Gordon to Khartoum."[14] As for Her Majesty herself, she was taking a close interest in the "Soudan difficulty," and was relieved that finally something was being done about it and the "best solution;" that is, Gordon, was being sent. In a thinly veiled swipe at the Gladstone government, she wrote to Sir Evelyn Wood, the *sirdar* or commander in chief of the Egyptian army: "Why this was not done long ago and why the right thing is never done until it is absolutely extorted from those who are in authority, is inexplicable to the Queen."[15] In this regard, for the queen at least, there would be much worse to come.

Gordon's ship arrived at Port Said on January 24. His original plan was to bypass Cairo altogether and go directly through the Suez Canal and the Red Sea to Suakin, then overland to Khartoum. He was met by Wood and one of his staff officers, Lt. Col. Charles Watson, at port and given a letter from Baring asking him to go to Cairo to consult about next steps and meet with the khedive. Watson, who had worked under Gordon in Equatoria ten years earlier, could not have been happier to see his old chief again. A few days before when Wood had informed him that Gordon was on his way out from London en route for Sudan, he had enthused, "That is the best thing I've heard for the last year."[16] Meantime, Gordon might have been inclined to ignore Baring's request had it not been for another letter given to him at that moment from his close friend, Gerald Graham, also in the Egyptian capital. Writing from Shepheard's Hotel—the epicenter of British and European social and political life in the Middle East—Graham implored Gordon to alter his plans: "My Dear Charlie, *Do* come to Cairo. Wood will tell you much better than I *why*. Throw over all personal feelings if you have any and act like yourself with straightforward directness."[17]

Graham's reference to "personal feelings" meant Gordon's antipathy toward Khedive Tewfik, whom he regarded as weak willed and responsible for allowing the gains formerly made against the slave trade in southern Sudan to wither since taking over for his deposed father. In light of the dual appeal made by Baring and Graham, however, Gordon changed his plans and proceeded to Cairo. He there met with Baring and then with Tewfik, an agreeable enough session during which he was given two firmans. The first proclaimed his reappointment as governor general of Sudan while the other—to be issued whenever Gordon thought appropriate—announced the independence of Sudan and the peaceful evacuation of the Egyptian garrisons.

Before departing for Khartoum Gordon encountered a ghost from his anti-slave-trade past: Zubair Rahmat, the exiled Sudanese slave boss whose son, Suleiman, had been executed five years earlier by Romolo Gessi acting under Gordon's sanction. Gordon made a quick, intuitive decision that

Zubair was the only man who could hold the rebellious Sudanese tribes together once the evacuation took place. In Gordon's view, as unsavory a man as Zubair was, he was the only one who had the necessary tribal network and political authority to best the Mahdi. On January 26 in a highly charged interview at the British agency in front of Baring, the Egyptian Prime Minister, Nubar Pasha, as well as other officials, Gordon and Zubair sparred for a short time over the manner and cause of Suleiman's death. Zubair's animosity was understandably sharp, but Gordon parried him and after Zubair had been dismissed told the officials assembled in the room why still he wanted him for the job. He was sure, said Gordon, that Zubair had "a capacity for government far beyond any other man in the Sudan. All the followers of the Mahdi would, I believe, leave the Mahdi on Zebeyr's [sic] approach, for the Mahdi's chiefs are ex-chiefs of Zebeyr [sic]."[18] Having just witnessed the snarling former slaver who seemed likely to kill Gordon if he had the chance, Baring simply could not accept that the two men could work together, even if it might result in the undercutting of the Mahdi's power. Given the circumstances, his position is understandable, although it would later change, and he and the council refused Gordon's request. Gordon described having a "mystic feeling" about Zubair's rightness for post-evacuation Sudan, but it did little to sway Baring.[19] "I have no confidence," he wrote later, "in opinions based on mystic feelings."[20] Zubair did not accompany Gordon to Khartoum.

Following a desultory dinner hosted by Baring, a bitterly disappointed Gordon departed Cairo that night. His plan to use Zubair, as risky as it would have been, seemed the best chance to install a successor government in Khartoum that might prevent Sudan from slipping permanently into extremist rule. Recognizing Gordon's subdued state of mind, a slightly apologetic Baring and some other officials saw him off at the railway station. The consul general's view of Gordon was changing for the better and he had just a few days earlier written to Gordon to say that he was "exceedingly glad" to know of his coming to Egypt. Baring told Gordon that once he was established at Khartoum it might be possible to send Zubair.[21] Gordon, slightly mollified by this unexpected news, headed south in anticipation of using the Nile route—"you will not hear much from me now," he wrote to Augusta—and arrived in Khartoum on February 18.[22]

Gordon read Baring's instructions during his trip to Khartoum, which directed him to evacuate Sudan keeping in mind the "saving of life and property" and to establish "some rough form of government which will prevent, so far as is possible, anarchy and confusion."[23] As he had mentioned in a letter to Lord Northbrook, the first lord of the admiralty and one of the four ministers in attendance at his war office interview, Gordon was confident that the "Mahdi's Kingdom will fall to pieces ere long."[24] Steaming upriver toward the heart of Mahdi-held territory with Stewart—whom he had already determined was "a capital fellow"—Gordon had no doubt that in time the Sudanese would rally to his call for a government composed of their own sultans based on the principles of just taxation and gradually enforced abolition.[25] He blamed the "weakness" of the Egyptian government for turning the favor of so many Sudanese to the Mahdi. Being back in the Sudan and on the way to his former capital, he wrote to Northbrook on February 1, was his "great reward." He lamented the Hicks disaster: "One can imagine what state his troops were in, after such a march with such men, worn out, dragging their useless guns," but as for himself, "I am very glad to go on this mission, and the people seem very glad."

If anything, Gordon was over sanguine about his return to the Sudan. He continued to believe that Zubair was the key to his plans and he remarked jauntily to Northbrook, "I like the plucky outspoken slave hunter and if [the] Government will let me I will have him back in the Soudan."[26] His brimming confidence, however, would cause him to make what many at the time and most historians since have considered a crucial mistake. In doing so, he went even against his own earlier stated position. As he neared the end of his journey to Khartoum, Gordon deliberated hard and then decided to make public the second firman given to him by the khedive. At Berber on February 15, he assembled the local officials, merchants, and Muslim *ulama* (scholars) and read the contents of the document to them, which stated that Sudan was to be made independent of Egypt and its troops evacuated. Gordon's intention in doing so was to encourage the petty sultans to build up their following based on a sense of Sudanese political honor over which, for the time being anyway, he would act as British overlord. In due course, once the Mahdi's power had been broken and the evacuation taken place, the country could look to just government and real independence under its own leaders.

The announcement's impact on many Sudanese was that of abandonment and surrender. At this juncture, he even tried to co-opt the Mahdi himself by offering to make him Sultan of Kordofan, the province where he was then encamped. The Mahdi naturally reacted with scorn to the peremptory nature of the offer, although as governor general it was Gordon's to make. In a long letter of reply to Gordon, the Mahdi called into question his political judgment, ridiculed his Christian faith, enjoined him to convert to Islam, and commanded him to remember that "I am the Expected Mahdi and I do not boast! I am the successor of God's Prophet and have no need of any sultanate, of Kordofan or anywhere else."[27]

Prior to making this offer to the Mahdi, Gordon remained resistant to the idea of jihad and the underlying religious nature of the *Mahdia*. Now it was becoming clearer to him that the Mahdi's motives were overwhelmingly theocratic and that he was inspiring his followers in a full-scale religious revolt. Gordon had attributed Sudanese unrest to misgovernment, and his direct dealings with the Mahdi confirmed that misgovernment by "infidels" (both Muslim and Christian) powered the Mahdi's rebellion and his committed *Ansar*. Despite the events at Berber, Gordon's arrival in Khartoum on February 18 was rapturous. The whole town, which had a population of more than forty thousand, nine thousand of who were troops, seemed to have come down to the river landing for the occasion. He waded through the exultant crowds who reached out to touch him and to kiss his feet, and surrounded by shouts of "Father" and "Sultan" he proceeded to a dais where he made a short speech. "I am glad to see you," Gordon began. "It is four years since I was here and the Sudan is miserable and I am miserable! And I want your assistance to put it right! I might have brought numbers of troops but I have come here without troops and we must ask Almighty God to look after the Sudan if no one else can."[28] He then ordered the gates to be flung open so passage in and out of the city could be made freely, burned the debt books, freed prisoners kept unjustly behind bars, and quickly formed a council of notables. The celebrations lasted throughout the night. As for Gordon's own estimation of his arrival in Khartoum, he wrote to the ever-loyal Augusta to say merely that he had been "well received."[29]

The task at hand was immediately both overwhelming and intense. Gordon was working from the assumption that eleven thousand people, both civilian and military, needed to be evacuated from the capital. To do so he had at his disposal a number of government steamers, which began to leave regularly before the end of February. He reorganized the defense of Khartoum, using Sudanese "Black" troops rather than the remaining Bashi-Bazouks, the hated Turkish irregulars, or what he viewed to be the unreliable Egyptians. He knew this policy would be risky, as he would lose some of the Sudanese to the Mahdi's sway, but he judged that the reward of having the Sudanese themselves defend their own capital out-weighed the risk. The Mahdi, encamped at El Obeid, southwest of Khartoum in Kordofan, had spies who kept him well informed about what Gordon was doing. Gordon's expectation of a siege was ever present. For the time being, he concluded that "there seems to be no chance of the Mahdi coming out of Obeid."[30] At the same time, he sent Colonel Stewart and Frank Power, correspondent for the *Times* and recently appointed British consul at Khartoum, to spread the firman's proclamations about independence and evacuation, and to reconnoiter upriver to report on the movements of the Mahdi and his forces. Wolseley advised that Gordon keep his own counsel and resist the urge to communicate constantly with Baring in Cairo. "My private advice," wrote Wolseley near the end of February, "Do not answer telegrams about your doings. Ask to be let alone. Results speak for themselves."[31]

Wolseley was prescient in this advice because despite Gordon reporting early in March that "we are getting on all right," a telegram sent to Cairo a week earlier was proving highly problematic.[32] In it, he had used the words "attack rebels" to describe Colonel Stewart's mission. His choice of expression was highly unfortunate but it did not reflect the intelligence-gathering nature of the Stewart expedition (and of another one, which was called off). The full text of the telegram, and a second one sent the same day, February 26, make clear Gordon's continuing pacific intentions, al-though after a month at Khartoum it seemed appropriate for him to show the Mahdi's rebels that he was willing to use force to ensure that the evacuation would be carried out unhindered. Unfortunately, Baring's trans-missions to London omitted certain words and intentions expressed by Gordon, and the impression left on the cabinet when it read "attack rebels" was one of a mission beginning to exceed its brief.[33]

Gordon's first month as governor general convinced him also about the absolute necessity of Zubair being sent to Khartoum as his successor. "I hope much from Zebehr's [sic] coming up," he wrote to Augusta.[34] He continued to pressure Baring on this point, about which the consul general now changed his mind and agreed, advising London that "Zobeir [sic] Pasha should be allowed to succeed Gordon. . . . I should think that delay would be injurious."[35] However, the problem for both men, at last allies—unlikely ones given their remaining personal antipathy—was that London had succumbed to intense pressure by the Anti-Slavery Society to ensure that Zubair not be allowed to leave Cairo. As far as they were concerned, sending the infamous slaver to Khartoum with the intention of making him ruler over Sudan once the evacuation was complete was unthinkable. Gordon, the anti-slaver extraordinaire, was hamstrung by the very society that had been his former champion.[36]

When the British government's decision reached Gordon early in March, he assumed it was absolute and concluded that without Zubair, the second part of his job, to ensure the transition to a Sudanese government that had a reasonable chance of success, was impossible. He would evacuate Sudan and leave the rest up to Egypt. As he wrote to Baring: "You must remember that, when evacuation is carried out, Mahdi will come down here and, by agents, will not let Egypt be quiet. Of course my duty is evacuation and the best I can for establishing a quiet government. The first I hope to accomplish. The second is a difficult task and concerns Egypt more than me. If Egypt is to be quiet, Mahdi must be smashed up."[37]

Again, Gordon's choice of words got him into trouble in London. In writing of the Mahdi having to be "smashed up" he was not declaring his considered plan of attack, but rather giving candid advice as to what Egypt may or may not choose to do. Unfortunately, the cabinet, especially Sir Charles Dilke, the president of the local government board and former under secretary for foreign affairs, and one of Gordon's interviewers at the hurried session on January 18, chose to interpret his position as needlessly aggressive and insubordinate of their authority. They were wrong on this point, and a full reading of the assorted telegrams that passed back and forth between Khartoum and Cairo and Cairo and London makes that clear. Nevertheless, the damage was done, and the perception that Gordon was acting independently and potentially recklessly was now a persistent one in London. One recognizes the politician's reflex of self-protection in Dilke's fantastic claim that in Gordon the cabinet was "dealing with a wild man under the influence of that climate of Central Africa which acts upon the sanest man like strong drink."[38]

Gordon, unaware of this soaring hyperbole in London and its potential ramifications, saw his situation clarified. Khartoum's telegraph line was cut in mid-March by the Mahdi's men. Gordon's direct link to Cairo and the outside world ended, and with it the anticipated siege of the city began.

Around the same time that Gordon's ability to send and receive telegrams was cut off, about three hundred miles to the northeast of Khartoum another drama was being played out on the Red Sea coast. At Suakin and then at Tamai, British troops sent from Egypt had lost and then won battles against the Mahdi's supporters, the fierce Hadendowa tribesmen, the so-called "Fuzzy Wuzzys" owing to their wildly matted hair and about which Kipling—"So 'ere's *to* you, Fuzzy-Wuzzy, at your 'ome in the Sowdan"—would marvel.[39] During the second engagement, Gerald Graham led his troops to victory and then sought to press forward to Berber and Khartoum, the only potentially useful thing about his sideshow campaign. Baring agreed with Graham's plan wholeheartedly, but London said no, insistent that Gordon could leave Khartoum if he chose to. The troops were withdrawn to Egypt. Assuming that the British would be not coming in force to relieve Khartoum, thousands of the Mahdi's followers swarmed into an area known as Halfaya just a few miles north of Khartoum on March 12. Gordon could hear their drums beating. "No human power can deliver us now," he wrote a short time later, "we are surrounded."[40]

The long months of siege commenced. For the next 320 days Khartoum was asphyxiated slowly as the Mahdi's forces ranged themselves ever closer around the beleaguered city, and inside its barricaded walls panic increased, food ran low, and money was exhausted. To remedy this last problem and enable a basic kind of commerce to continue, Gordon printed small currency notes, signed in his own hand.[41] He endeavored to keep up morale by having bands play regularly and he inspected the defenses and the garrison constantly to keep himself in full view of the townspeople. "We are all right," he wrote just after the siege began, "the enemy has established himself some 6000 strong. . . . We are well off for food, and the people are in good spirits . . . We could go on for months."[42] This bit of bravado on

Gordon's part is understandable, since all communication with the outside world now was entrusted to spies who took their lives in their hands to slip through the Mahdi's lines and proceed downriver to a reachable Egyptian-controlled town. If caught en route, such a sanguine report of the state of Khartoum just might give the Mahdi reason to pause in his relentless campaign to starve the city into surrender.

Throughout the spring, summer, and early autumn of 1884 Gordon was in his element in the besieged town. A lifetime's experience leading troops, of administration and organization, and self-sufficiency, all came to the fore. He was determined to withstand the Mahdi, in whatever form—"he is not likely to stop short"—and hold the city until the British government saw no other choice but to relieve it.[43] He did not know that in London, Granville and others continued to resist his call for the sending of a British force to Khartoum. Granville was supported staunchly by Gladstone who, in May, had responded to strong denunciation by both the press and by the opposition Tories. The conflict began when Gladstone had risen in parliament and rather remarkably expressed a certain sympathy for the Mahdists, stating that, "Yes; these people are struggling to be free; and they are struggling rightly to be free."[44] The prime minister may have been expressing ideas resulting from a reasonable mingling of his former Midlothian internationalist mindset with the Sudan situation, but few others could see it. The queen, who "trembles for General Gordon's safety," was almost beside herself with frustration. "For the honour of the Government and the nation," she wrote furiously to Gladstone, "he must not be abandoned. . . . The Queen has no confidence in Lord Granville; he is as weak as water."[45]

At the war office, Wolseley was likewise incensed with the inexplicable resistance to relieving Khartoum, saving Gordon, and striking a blow for the honor of the nation. The government's continuing blind spot in the affair, suggests Colin Matthew persuasively, was that Gladstone and the cabinet did not sense this fact of national honor keenly enough. On some of the complex issues of the geo-political situation they may have been right. Gordon could be a difficult and willful man, but the revolt in Sudan called for a higher grade of statesmanship than that being practiced by the contemporary liberal government. "They took their stand on details," observes Matthew, ". . . when what was really at issue was presentation and image."[46]

Wolseley's call for action was the loudest. At the end of May, Berber fell to the Mahdi and even the government could not pretend that Gordon was not truly surrounded and all escape routes blocked. Shortly thereafter, and faced still with cabinet inaction, Wolseley wrote to Gordon and, in a letter that actually made it through to him, denounced Gladstone harshly, calling him a "craven politician." He enjoined Gordon to "Hold out to the last. Be of good courage. I have no fear for you: the God in whom you trust will not desert you even though you be deserted by an infamous Minister."[47]

On August 5, under intense pressure from Hartington, who threatened to resign and had supported going to Gordon's assistance but had been overruled, Gladstone chose finally to act. The government authorized £300,000 for a relief expedition, over which Wolseley would have command. A month later he was in Cairo. Upon hearing the news Gordon, while pleased, was not unremittingly so. He bridled at the "imputation that the projected expedition has come to *relieve me*." National honor with respect to Egypt was at stake, he believed, and always had been, and to safeguard it the government was sending a second relief expedition: "*I was relief expedition No. 1.*"[48]

On September 12, three days after Wolseley arrived at Cairo, Gordon sent Colonel Stewart, Frank Power, and some others in a steamer downriver in an attempt to reestablish dependable communication with Baring in Egypt. The mission was extremely dangerous. The Mahdi's men lined much of the Nile's banks, and were poised to attack the steamer mercilessly. Stewart did not want to leave Gordon alone in Khartoum, but he was ordered to go. Gordon entrusted to him various documents including his journal. Alas, the fear that they would not make it through was realized. The steamer, *Abbas*, ran aground on a rock. The stranded men accepted the invitation of a local sheikh to have dinner and take shelter. Trusting too much in their host's traditional Arab hospitality they went forward unarmed. Shortly thereafter they were ambushed and murdered, although word of the capture of the *Abbas*—"a terrible blow"—did not reach Gordon until late October.[49]

After much delay in the arrival of troops and equipment, and disagreements over the choice of routes (the Nile, or the Red Sea and then overland) Wolseley finally had set out from Cairo on September 27. From that date it took an agonizing four months before a steamer with an advance party of only twenty troops reached Khartoum.

Throughout this period Gordon continued to do the things that had helped sustain the besieged city since March. He remained convinced that he would "scramble through this ordeal," but by December food stocks were close to exhausted, the people were wild with hunger and fear, and the troops were in no fit state to resist a direct assault by the Mahdi's Ansar.[50] Since about the end of October the Mahdi had been encamped near Khartoum, across the White Nile near Omdurman. Neighborhood skirmishes erupted occasionally, but mostly both sides played a waiting game. The city's fortifications were mined heavily, and were supported by outlying forts, such as that at Omdurman. Though food was scarce, ammunition was not and the air crackled with artillery and gunfire and the occasional explosion. Gordon's hair had turned mostly white with the strain. He smoked incessantly, paced the rooftop of his palace redoubt—"I am on *tenter hooks*!"—and scribbled daily in his journal. In it, he insisted that he would "stay here, and fall with the town."[51] On December 14, still unsure whether a relief force was close at hand or not, he made his last journal entry: "Now MARK THIS, if the Expeditionary Force, and I ask for no more than two hundred men, does not come in ten days, *the town may fall*; and I have done my best for the honour of our country. Good bye."[52] That same day he wrote the beloved Augusta: "This may be the last letter you will receive from me, for we are on our last legs, owing to the delay of the Expedition . . . I am quite happy, thank God, & like Lawrence [Sir Henry of Indian Mutiny fame], I have '*tried* to do my duty.'"[53]

In the six weeks of silence that ensued only one brief message reached Wolseley from Gordon about what was happening at Khartoum. Wolseley had predicted earlier that the relief expedition would reach the city early in November.[54] It was more than a month later and the long, tortuous passage south continued, "a slowness of progress which bespoke failure almost from the start," a retired infantryman who was on the expedition wrote years later.[55] Gordon's message, dated December 14, stated that Khartoum was "all right." Wolseley received it on December 31 at Korti, and based on the verbal report that accompanied it decided to send two columns, one up the Nile to retake Berber and the other, principally a Camel Corps, to cross the desert direct to Metemma on the Nile and thence to the capital. These decisions and their consequent execution took time, which now early in the New Year 1885, Gordon did not have.

Since receiving a letter from the Mahdi in late October in which he gloated over the deaths of Stewart and Power, taunted Gordon about needing to be saved by the British, and exhorted him to convert to Islam, a final violent climacteric between them was inevitable.[56] As Gordon remarked at the time: "It is impossible for me to have any more words with Mohammed Achmed, only lead."[57] On January 5, the besieged government fort at Omdurman surrendered to the Ansar, which now numbered as many as sixty thousand.[58] Over the ensuing three weeks not much is known of Gordon's activities. On January 18, the desert column sent by Wolseley won a decisive victory over a force of Ansar at Abu Klea. In the Mahdi's camp across the Nile, which Gordon could see through his rooftop telescope, public lamentation ensued over the defeat and loss of life. Gordon was heartened by the fact that this display must mean that the relief force was close. A week later, on January 25, there was still no sign of its expected smoke-belching steamers. An interminable slowness gripped the would-be saviors of Khartoum. The two officers who were to have commanded the final push to the city had been killed, one at Abu Klea, and the other two days later. The result was that Sir Charles Wilson was given command. He had never had operational command of troops on campaign before, and used up two days in over-cautious reconnaissance before setting out up the Nile from Metemma on the January 24. Back on December 13, in Gordon's penultimate journal entry, he had written in exasperation: "It is inexplicable, this delay … one hundred men are all that we require, just to show themselves … this is not asking much but it must happen *at once*; or it will, as usual, be too late."[59]

The Mahdi chose this moment to launch his final attack on the capital. The seasonally receding Nile had exposed a narrow ridge of land that created a passageway through to the city walls. One of Gordon's officers turned traitor and went over to the Mahdi, informing him of this breech in Khartoum's defenses. Early in the morning of January 26, the weakened city was penetrated by the Ansar, who controlled it an hour later. That fateful hour was a murderous one, and there would be thirteen more like it until the Mahdi finally called off the indiscriminate slaughter and rapine that afternoon. As many as ten thousand men, women and children, one-quarter of Khartoum's population, were brutally killed that day, the most prized among them being Gordon himself.[60]

At the sound of the attack, Gordon came down from his top floor room at the palace. No one knows for certain how he died. Various eyewitness reports have him defending himself before being cut down; others have him descending the palace staircase calmly and facing his fate; G.W. Joy's iconic painting depicts him standing defiantly at the top of the staircase on the verge of being run through with a spear; another account tells of him being set upon by a group of emirs armed with spears and swords who knocked him down and then "rushed in and cutting at the prostrate body with their swords must have killed him in a few seconds."[61] However it happened, his body was never found. Following Gordon's death, his head was cut off and taken to the victorious Mahdi's camp. One of the prisoners held there was Rudolf Slatin, the Austrian former governor of conquered Darfur. The dead man's head was brought to him before the bloody prize was put on display for the frenzied jihadists. "His blue eyes were half-opened," Slatin wrote later, "the mouth was perfectly natural; the hair of his head and his short whiskers were almost quite white." Asked if this was not "the head of your uncle, the unbeliever," Slatin replied, "What of it? A brave soldier, who fell at his post. Happy is he to have fallen; his sufferings are over."[62]

Word of the fall of Khartoum and Gordon's almost certain death reached London on February 5. Sadness for a slain hero turned almost immediately to anger. Gladstone was hissed at in public and given a new nickname: the GOM (Grand Old Man) became the MOG (Murderer of Gordon). Wolseley, still at Korti, wrote to Gordon's brother Henry describing the "whole Khartoum business" as a "nightmare" and that "Mr. Gladstone has much to answer for to our nation . . ."[63] The Queen continued in her outrage: "These news from Khartoum are frightful ... pray, but have little hope, that brave Gordon may yet be alive."[64] Meanwhile, Charles Wilson, the man who had arrived at the ruined and still-smoking city on January 28, two days after its fall and subsequent occupation by the Mahdi's men, wrote Henry to say that "it was a cruel disappointment to reach Khartoum on your brother's birthday and find I was too late."[65] Gordon had been right: Khartoum's relief had come too late, but for the ultimate soldier of empire, after a lifetime of service, no better end could have been sought.

Notes

Preface

1. Lytton Strachey, *Eminent Victorians* (London: Chatto and Windus, 1918).

2. See, for example, Bernard Allen, *Gordon and the Sudan* (London: Macmillan, 1931), 83–96. Recently, in a casual conversation with someone who knows his way around history, I mentioned that I was working on a biography of Gordon. "Oh, that religious fanatic!" was his first and only response.

3. Michael Asher, *Khartoum: The Ultimate Imperial Adventure* (London: Penguin, 2006), 406–7.

Chapter 1: To The Army Born: Woolwich and Wales

1. Gordon's statue now stands on the Victoria Embankment, very near the old war office, a building he frequented and visited last on the January afternoon in 1885 when he left for Sudan for the last time.

2. Quoted in *The Journals of Major-General C. G. Gordon C. B. at Kartoum*. A. Egmont Hake, ed. (London: Kegan Paul, Trench, 1885), 6.

3. Ibid.

4. Arnold, famously, was another of the "Eminent Victorians" skewered by Strachey.

5. See J. R. de S. Honey, *Tom Brown's Universe: The Development of the English Public School in the Nineteenth Century* (New York: Quadrangle, 1977).

6. Quoted in John Pollock, *Gordon: The Man Behind the Legend* (London: Constable, 1993), 17.

7. Ibid., 13.

8. The precise date is not known because a fire later destroyed the Royal Military Academy's records.

9. See, for example, John H. Waller, *Gordon of Khartoum: The Saga of a Victorian Hero* (New York: Atheneum, 1988), chapter 1.

10. At Oxford and Cambridge undergraduates would (and do still) walk across a dining table in order to reach a desired seat.

11. His French must not have been too bad because he later conversed and corresponded in the language.

12. See Bernard M. Allen, *Gordon and the Sudan* (London: Macmillan, 1931), chapter 1.

13. After Gordon's death, the Royal Engineers commissioned a statue of him on camelback. First exhibited at the Royal Academy in London in 1890, it was then taken to the Brompton barracks where it stands, just inside the main gate, to this day. A second, identical statue stood formerly in Khartoum, but since Sudanese independence in 1956, it has been located on the grounds of Gordon's School in Woking, Surrey.

14. The historiography on the Crimean War is large and becoming larger. See, for example, Trevor Royle's recent, *Crimea: the Great Crimean War, 1854–1856* (London: Palgrave Macmillan, 2004).

15. See David Bebbington, *Evangelicalism in Modern Britain: A History from the 1730s to the 1980s* (London: Unwin Hyman/Routledge, 1989).

16. Quoted in Pollock, *Gordon*, 27.

17. Ibid.

18 "Crimean War Notebook," General Gordon Papers, GB165-0120, St. Antony's College, Oxford, Middle East Centre Archives.

Chapter 2: Crimea and Beyond: Youthful Soldiering and Surveying

1. See J. B. Conacher, *The Aberdeen Coalition 1852–1855: A Study in Mid-Nineteenth Century Party Politics* (Cambridge: Cambridge University Press, 1968).

2. See, for example, John R. Davis, *The Great Exhibition* (Stroud: Sutton, 1999). Also, Jeffrey A. Auerbach, *The Great Exhibition of 1851: A Nation on Display* (New Haven, CT: Yale University Press, 1999).

3. Quoted in Cecil Woodham-Smith, *Queen Victoria: Her Life and Times*

1819–1861 (London: Hamish Hamilton, 1984), 315.

4. Charles Dickens, *Dombey and Son*, Alan Horsman, ed. (Oxford: Oxford University Press, 2001), 2.

5. Clive Ponting, *The Crimean War* (London: Chatto and Windus, 2004), 5.

6. Quoted in Pollock, *Gordon*, 32.

7. See Royle, *Crimea*, part II, chapter 4. Also, Lynn McDonald, ed. *The Collected Works of Florence Nightingale* (Waterloo, ON: Wilfrid Laurier University Press, 2001).

8. "Crimean War Notebook," Gordon Papers, St. Antony's College, Oxford.

9. Ibid.

10. Pollock, *Gordon*, 286. Quoted in Waller, *Gordon of Khartoum*, 369.

11. BL Add. 52389 f. 29 (June 12, 1855).

12. Alastair Massie, *The National Army Museum Book of the Crimean War* (London: Sidgwick & Jackson, 2004), 202.

13. Ibid., 207.

14. Ibid., 207–8.

15. Quoted in *The Panmure Papers*, George Brisbane Douglas and George Ramsay, eds., 2 vols (London: Hodder & Stoughton, 1908), vol. I, 289.

16. Quoted in Albert Seaton, *The Crimean War: A Russian Chronicle* (London: Batsford, 1977), 196.

17. Ponting, *The Crimean War*, 291.

18. Pollock, *Gordon*, 35.

19. Paul Fussell, *The Great War and Modern Memory* (Oxford: Oxford University Press, 1975), chapter two.

20. Quoted in Pollock, *Gordon*, 36.

21. Quoted in Lord Elton, *General Gordon* (London: Collins, 1954), 32.

22. BL Add. 33222, f. 7. (September 10, 1855).

23. Quoted in Pollock, *Gordon*, 37.

24. Ibid., 37–38.

25. Ibid., 40.

26. BL Add. 52389, f. 163 (November 17, 1858).

27. Quoted in Charles Chenevix Trench, *The Road to Khartoum: A Life of General Charles Gordon* (New York: Norton, 1979), 23.

28. Quoted in Elton, *General Gordon*, 39.

Chapter 3: China: To Wear the Yellow Jacket

1. Jasper Ridley, *Lord Palmerston* (New York: E. P Dutton, 1971), 539–40.

2. Jurgen Osterhammel, "Britain and China, 1842–1914," in *The Oxford History of the British Empire*, vol. III, *The Nineteenth Century*, edited by Andrew Porter (Oxford: Oxford University Press, 1999), 146.

3. Franz Michael, *The Taiping Rebellion*, vol. I (Seattle: University of Washington Press, 1966), 199.

4. The best and most recent study of Hong and the Taiping Rebellion is by Jonathan D. Spence, *God's Chinese Son: The Taiping Heavenly Kingdom of Hong Xiuquan* (New York: Norton, 1996).

5. See J. S. Gregory, *Great Britain and the Taipings* (London: Routledge & Kegan Paul, 1969).

6. Quoted in Pollock, *Gordon*, 50.

7. Samuel Mossman, ed., *General Gordon's Private Diary of His Exploits in China*. (London: Sampson Low, 1885), 37, 45.

8. Some of this booty was sent to the Royal Engineers' depot at Chatham where it is on view today in special display cases dedicated to Gordon.

9. BL Add. 52389, f. 218 (October 25, 1860). Quoted in Waller, *Gordon of Khartoum*, 61.

10. See John King Fairbank, *China: A New History* (Cambridge, MA: Belknap/Harvard University Press, 201–5.

11. See Caleb Carr, *The Devil Soldier: The Story of Frederick Townsend Ward* (New York: Random House, 1992).

12. BL Add. 52403, f. 19 (October 10, 1885).

13. Mossman, ed., *General Gordon's Private Diary*, 66.

14. BL Add. 52386, f. 5 (January 25, 1863).

15. Mossman, ed., *General Gordon's Private Diary*, 162.

16. Spence, *God's Chinese Son*, ch. 21.

17. Fairbank, *China*, 216.

18. The corn-colored cane is another of the many Gordon artifacts on display at the Royal Engineers Museum, Chatham.

19. Pollock, *Gordon*, 67.

20. Gordon named one of the children orphaned by the war "Quincey" and saw to it that he received an education in Shanghai. He later became chief of police on the Shanghai-Nanking Railway.

21. Mossman, ed. *General Gordon's Private Diary*, 195.

22. Ibid., 251–52.

23. Waller, *Gordon of Khartoum*, 104.

24. BL Add. 52386, f. 143 (December 15, 1863).

25. Mossman, ed., *General Gordon's Private Diary*, 259.

26. Spence, *God's Chinese Son*, 331.

27. The Yellow Jacket today can be viewed at the Royal Engineers Museum, Chatham.

28. *The Times* (London), August 5, 1864.

29. BL Add. 52389, f. 49 (November 17, 1864).

30. Michael, *The Taiping Rebellion*, vol. I, 171.

Chapter 4: The Years Between: Gravesend and Galatz

1. Pollock, *Gordon*, 100.

2. Ibid.

3. Ibid.

4. Hake, *The Story of Chinese Gordon* (London: Remington, 1884), 7.

5. Quoted in Octavia Freese, *More About Gordon* (London: Bentley, 1894), 18.

6. Quoted in Sir Richard Harrison, *A Life in the British Army* (London: Macmillan, 1908), 119.

7. See, for example, Richard Aldous, *The Lion and the Unicorn: Gladstone vs Disraeli* (London: Hutchinson, 2006), 96.

8. See Bebbington, *Evangelicalism in Modern Britain*.

9. 2 Corinthians 5:17

10. Waller, *Gordon of Khartoum*, 119.

11. BL Add. 51291, ff. 34-35 (June 12, 1866).

12. 1 John 4:15.

13. Quoted in *Cornhill Magazine* (April 1917), 236.

14. Quoted in Freese, *More About Gordon*, 6.

15. The Reverend F. E. Freese, "Gordon, 1867–1885," General Gordon Papers, St. Antony's College, Oxford.

16. Quoted in Pollock, *Gordon*, 115.

17. Waller, *Gordon of Khartoum*, 129.

18. See, for example, H. E. Wortham, *Gordon: An Intimate Portrait* (London: George Harrap, 1933), 32.

19. *Oxford Dictionary of National Biography*, vol. 22, H. C. G. Matthew and Brian Harrison, eds. (Oxford: Oxford University Press, 2004), 865.

20. BL Add. 51292, f. 165 (April 17, 1880). Quoted in Chenevix-Trench, *The Road to Khartoum*, 64.

21. Quoted in Waller, *Gordon of Khartoum*, 130.

22. Eighteen such responses are contained in BL Add. 52394, f. 98.

23. BL Add. 52394, ff. 66–67 (November 25, 1868).

24. Quoted in Pollock, *Gordon*, 125.

25. Quoted in Brian Thompson, *Imperial Vanities: The Adventures of the Baker Brothers and Gordon of Khartoum* (London: HarperCollins, 2002), 118.

26. Quoted in Pollock, *Gordon*, 131.

27. Sir Samuel Baker, *Ismailia*, 2 vols. (London: Macmillan, 1874), vol. II, 513.

28. Quoted in Waller, *Gordon of Khartoum*, 137–38.

29. M. A. Gordon, ed. *Letters of General C. G. Gordon to His Sister* (London: Macmillan, 1888), 69.

30. General Gordon Papers, File 2, f. 1, St. Antony's College, Oxford.

Chapter 5: Sudan I: Exploration, Slavery, and Abolition

1. Viscount Milner, *England in Egypt*, 13th ed. (New York: H. Ferlig, 1970), 13–14.

2. See, for example, John Hanning Speke, *Journey of the Discovery of the Source of the Nile; Chiefly Illustrated from Drawings by James Grant* (Mineola, NY: Dover Publications, 1996), and Michael Brander, *The Perfect Victorian Hero, Samuel White Baker* (Edinburgh: Mainstream, 1982). For a modern-day account of this quintessential Victorian adventure, see Christopher Ondaatje, *Journey to the Source of the Nile* (Toronto: HarperCollins, 1998).

3. Quoted in Sir John Adye, *Recollections of a Military Life*, (London: Macmillan, 1895), 274.

4. Quoted in Pollock, *Gordon*, 136.

5. George Birkbeck Hill, ed., *Colonel Gordon in Central Africa 1874–1879: From Original Letters and Documents* (London: Thomas de la Rue & Co., 1881), 118.

6. Quoted in Waller, *Gordon of Khartoum*, 168.

7. Hill, ed., *Colonel Gordon in Central Africa*, 121.

8. General Gordon Papers, St. Antony's College, Oxford, File 1, f. 2 (August 3, 1874).

9. Gordon, ed., *Letters of General C.G. Gordon*, 91.

10. BL Add. 51293, f. 23 (March 28, 1874).

11. Charles Chaille-Long, *The Three Prophets* (New York: Appleton, 1884), and *My Life on Four Continents* (New York: Hutchison, 1912).

12. Hill, ed., *Colonel Gordon in Central Africa*, 130. See Stephen Neill, *A History of Christian Missions* (Markham, ON: Penguin, 1987).

13. General Gordon Papers, St. Antony's College, Oxford, Gordon to Octavia Freese, May 2, 1876. See, also, Romolo Gessi Pasha, *Seven Years in the Soudan* (London: Sampson Low, Marston & Co., 1892).

14. Ibid., 177–79. Also, BL Add. 52395A, which is the special volume containing Gordon's expedition notebook. It is in very poor shape and, in many places, impossible to read.

15. BL Add. 51303, f. 50 (February 6, 1876). Later, Emin would become governor of Equatoria and a prominent figure in the history of European imperialism in North Africa. See, for example, Stanhope White, *Lost Empire on the Nile: H.M. Stanley, Emin Pasha and the Imperialists* (London: Hale, 1969).

16. Hill, ed., *Colonel Gordon in Central Africa*, 188.

17. Ibid., 194.

18. Ibid., 182.

19. *The Times* (London), December 29, 1876.

20. Gordon, ed., *Letters of General C.G. Gordon*, 104.

21. Hill, ed., *Colonel Gordon in Central Africa*, 211.

22. BL Add. 51305, ff. 87–8 (February 1, 1877).

23. Hill, ed., *Colonel Gordon in Central Africa*, 212.

24. Gordon, ed., *Letters of General C.G. Gordon*, 104–5.

25. *The Times* (London), July 21, 1877.

26. Hill, ed., *Colonel Gordon in Central Africa*, 231.

27. Ibid., 229.

28. Ibid., 230–31.

29. Ibid., 232–33.

30. Quoted in Allen, *Gordon and the Sudan*, 113.

31. Gordon was an accomplished bluffer. One of his friends, Sir John Cowell, told Queen Victoria that Gordon's "choice Arabic" when confronting Suleiman in the middle of the desert included a threat to order up the British fleet! Pollock, *Gordon*, 152.

32. The Dara episode and quotations are found in Hill, ed., *Colonel Gordon in Central Africa*, 271–77.

33. National Archives, Cromer Papers FO/638/2/p. 217 (T/S).

34. Quoted in Allen, *Gordon and the Sudan*, 133.

35. Quoted in Pollock, *Gordon*, 157.

36. BL Add. 51295, f. 96 (September 23, 1878).

37. Hill, ed., *Colonel Gordon in Central Africa*, 338.

38. Ibid., 340.

39. Gessi Pasha, *Seven Years in the Soudan*, 314.

40. Ibid., 323.

41. BL Add. 51305, ff. 98, 102 (June 28 and July 1, 1879).

42. Hill, ed., *Colonel Gordon in Central Africa*, 407.

43. Ibid., 402.

44. BL Add. 51304, ff. 100, 84 (October 27, 1879).

45. Hill, ed., *Colonel Gordon in Central Africa*, 411.

46. Ibid., 412.

47. *The Times* (London), January 22, 1880.

Chapter 6: A Roving Commission

1. See James L. Newman, *Imperial Footprints: Henry Morton Stanley's African Journeys* (Dulles, VA: Potomac Books, 2006), and Tim Jeal, *Stanley: The Impossible Life of Africa's Greatest Explorer* (London: Faber & Faber, 2007). See, also, Adam Hochschild, *King Leopold's Ghost: A Story of Greed, Terror, and Heroism in Central Africa* (Boston: Houghton Mifflin, 1998).

2. Quoted in Waller, *Gordon of Khartoum*, 254.

3. *Daily News* (London), June 1, 1880.

4. See C. Brad Faught, "An Imperial Prime Minister? W.E. Gladstone and India, 1880-1885," in *The Journal of the Historical Society*, vol. VI, no. 4 (December 2006), 555-78.

5. Gordon, ed., *Letters of General C.G. Gordon*, 157-59. BL Add. 52390, f. 48 (June 7, 1880).

6. Quoted in Pollock, *Gordon*, 192.

7. BL Add. 51304, ff. 118-21 (July 2, 1881).

8. Gordon, ed. *Letters of General C.G. Gordon*, 158.

9. Ibid.

10. Quoted in Pollock, *Gordon*, 195.

11. Ibid.

12. Roy Jenkins, *Gladstone* (London: Macmillan, 1995), 290.

13. BL Add. 44467, ff. 43-7 (November 30, 1880).

14. Gordon, ed., *Letters of General C.G. Gordon*, 161.

15. David Northrup, "Migration from Africa, Asia, and the South Pacific," in *The Oxford History of the British Empire*, vol. III, 88-91.

16. Pollock, *Gordon*, 228--33; Waller, *Gordon of Khartoum*, 270.

17. Gordon, ed., *Letters of General C.G. Gordon*, 196.

18. Leonard Thompson, *Survival in Two Worlds: Moshoeshoe of Lesotho, 1786-1870* (Oxford: Oxford University Press, 1975), 297

19. Quoted in Elton, *Gordon of Khartoum*, 257.

20. Gordon, ed., *Letters of General C.G. Gordon*, 210.

21. BL Add. 51311.

22. Gordon, ed., *Letters of General C.G. Gordon*, 219.

23. Ibid., 220. BL Add. 51308.

24. Pollock, *Gordon*, 258.

Chapter 7: Sudan II: Death in the Desert

1. Gordon, ed., *Letters of General C.G. Gordon*, 280.

2. BL Add. 52388, f. 135 (January 4, 1884).

3. *Pall Mall Gazette*, January 9, 1884; *The Times*, January 10, 1884.

4. Thompson, *Imperial Vanities*, 219.

5. Gordon, ed., *Letters of General C.G. Gordon*, 282. BL Add. 56451, f. 169 (January 15, 1884).

6. BL Add. 52402, ff. 152–53 (September 6, 1885).

7. Allen, *Gordon and the Sudan*, 221–22.

8. Roger Owen, *Lord Cromer: Victorian Imperialist, Edwardian Proconsul* (Oxford: Oxford University Press, 2004), 191–93; Allen, ibid, 226.

9. Quoted in John Morley, *Life of Gladstone*, vol. II (London: Macmillan, 1922), 390.

10. Allen, *Gordon and the Sudan*, 227–34.

11. Quoted in Wilfrid Scawen Blunt, *Gordon at Khartoum: Being a Personal Narrative of Events* (London: Stephen Swift, 1891), 512.

12. Pollock, *Gordon*, 273.

13. Gordon, ed., *Letters of General C.G. Gordon*, 282.

14. *Pall Mall Gazette*, (January 21, 1884.)

15. Christopher Hibbert, ed., *Queen Victoria in her Letters and Journals* (Markham, ON: Penguin, 1985), 284.

16. BL Add. 51301, ff. 184–200 (February 10, 1884).

17. BL Add. 52388, ff. 145–46 (January 23, 1884).

18. Quoted in Chenevix-Trench, *The Road to Khartoum*, 213.

19. Ibid.

20. Lord Cromer, *Modern Egypt*, vol. I (New York: Macmillan, 1908), 459.

21. BL Add. 52388, f. 142 (January 22, 1884).

22. Gordon, ed., *Letters of General C.G. Gordon*, 282.

23. BL Add. 52388, f. 144 (January 22, 1884).

24. BL Add. 43573, f. 89 (January 17, 1884).

25. Ibid., f. 93 (January 20, 1884).

26. Ibid., f. 98 (February 1, 1884).

27. Quoted in Fergus Nicoll, *The Mahdi of Sudan and the Death of General Gordon* (Stroud: Sutton, 2004), 223–24.

28. Quoted in Pollock, *Gordon*, 288.

29. BL Add. 51298, f. 179 (February 22, 1884).

30. Ibid., f. 181 (February 26, 1884).

31. General Gordon Papers, St. Antony's College, Oxford, Middle East Centre, GB 165-0120, File 4, f. 13 (February 21, 1884).

32. BL Add. 51298, f. 183 (March 5, 1884).

33. Allen, *Gordon and the Sudan*, 278–81.

34. Gordon, ed., *Letters of General C.G. Gordon*, 287.

35. BL Add. 56451, f. 13 (March 4, 1884).

36. Pollock, Gordon, 293.

37. BL Add. 56451, f. 14 (March 5, 1884). Quoted in Allen, *Gordon and the Sudan*, 282.

38. Allen, ibid., 285.

39. Rudyard Kipling, "Fuzzy-Wuzzy" (1890).

40. BL Add. 51300, f. 29 (April 30, 1884).

41. BL Add. 42711, f. 138.

42. BL Add. 51298, f. 185 (March 15, 1884).

43. BL Add. 56451, f. 19 (March 31, 1884).

44. Hansard, 288. 55 (May 12, 1884).

45. Hibbert, ed., *Queen Victoria*, 284–85.

46. H.C.G. Matthew, *Gladstone 1809–1898* (Oxford: Clarendon Press, 1997), 398.

47. Quoted in Pollock, *Gordon*, 301.

48. A. Egmont Hake, ed., *The Journals of Major-General C.G. Gordon, C.B. at Kartoum* (London: Kegan Paul, Trench, 1885), 93.

49. Ibid., 272.

50. BL Add. 51298, f. 188 (October 12, 1884).

51. BL Add. 44630, f. 1 (December 14, 1884). Hake, ed., The Journals, 307.

52. Hake, ed., ibid., 395.

53. BL Add. 51298, f. 193 (December 14, 1884).

54. BL Add. 43923, f. 175 (April 8, 1884).

55. W. Cyprian Bridge, "The Gordon Relief Expedition," Royal United Service Institution Essay, January 25, 1933. Old Gordonians Association collection, Gordon's School.

56. Nicoll, *The Mahdi of Sudan*, 243–44.

57. Quoted in Waller, *Gordon of Khartoum*, 405.

58. Nicoll, *The Mahdi of Sudan*, 243.

59. Hake, ed., *The Journals*, 394.

60. Asher, *Khartoum*, 261–67.

61. General Gordon Papers, St. Antony's College, Oxford, File 4, f. 16 (anonymous author, n.d.).

62. Rudolf Slatin, *Fire and Sword in the Sudan: A Personal Narrative of Fighting and Serving the Dervishes 1879–1895* (London: Edward Arnold, 1930), 206.

63. BL Add. 52401, ff. 73–4 (March 11, 1885).

64. Hibbert, ed., *Queen Victoria*, 289.

65. BL Add. 52401, f. 71 (March 11,1885).

Bibliographic Note

Any modern study of the life of Gordon should begin with the source material contained within the forty-five volume main collection of the Gordon Papers housed at the British Library in London. Letters, memoranda, documents, maps, and ephemera that span most of Gordon's life make it the most comprehensive cache of research material for studying the man. In addition to this collection another forty-one volumes are housed at the British Library in which letters from Gordon to various correspondents can be found. His letter writing was so prolific, and the number of correspondents so wide, that other significant collections exist elsewhere, including the Royal Engineers Museum, Chatham, St. Antony's College, Oxford, Middle East Centre, Cambridge University Library, Durham University Library, and the Boston Public Library.

An abundance of Gordon printed primary material also exists. The most important of these is his Khartoum diary edited by A. Egmont Hake, *The Journals of Major-General C.G. Gordon, C.B. at Kartoum* (London: Kegan Paul & Trench, 1885). *General Gordon's Private Diary of His Exploits in China* (London: Low, 1885) edited by Samuel Mossman, documents Gordon's Chinese period. On correspondence with his family see the volume edited by his sibling, M.A. Gordon, ed., *Letters of General C.G. Gordon to His Sister* (London: Macmillan, 1888).

Since 1884 many biographies and shorter sketches of Gordon have been written. A. Egmont Hake wrote one of the first, publishing *The Story of Chinese Gordon* (London: Remington) in 1884-85. Throughout the twentieth century at least eight substantial studies of Gordon's life were published The most accurate of these are by Bernard Allen, *Gordon and the Sudan* (London: Macmillan, 1931), Lord Elton, *General Gordon* (London:

Collins, 1954), Charles Chenevix Trench, *The Road to Khartoum: A Life of General Charles Gordon* (New York: Norton, 1979), John H. Waller, *Gordon of Khartoum: The Saga of a Victorian Hero* (New York: Atheneum, 1988), and John Pollock, *Gordon: The Man Behind the Legend* (London: Constable, 1993). Lytton Strachey's profile of Gordon in *Eminent Victorians* (London: Chatto & Windus, 1918), while superbly written, popular, and influential, was composed without serious reference to the Gordon source material and therefore cannot be considered a work of historical accuracy.

Area studies of China and the Sudan are essential for putting Gordon's activities there in a wider historical perspective. Jonathan D. Spence's, *God's Chinese Son: The Taiping Heavenly Kingdom of Hong Xiuquan* (New York: Norton, 1996) offers a full account of the Taiping Rebellion. J.S. Gregory provided a nuanced study of the British role in the Rebellion is provided in his book, *Great Britain and the Taipings* (London: Routledge & Kegan Paul, 1969). The best single volume general history of China, which includes an examination of the Taiping Rebellion, is by John King Fairbank, *China: A New History* (Cambridge, MA: The Belknap Press of Harvard University Press, 1992).

For Gordon's other major field of action, Africa, Robert O. Collins offers a detailed overview of colonial Sudan in *Egypt and the Sudan* (Englewood Cliffs, NJ: Prentice-Hall, 1967). A good general account of Sudan's history is provided by P.M. Holt, *A History of the Sudan: From the Coming of Islam to the Present Day*, 5th ed. (New York: Longman, 2000). The British period in Sudan's past is examined comprehensively in Peter Mansfield, *The British in Egypt* (New York: Macmillan, 1971).

Histories of the British Empire are numerous. Some of the best of those published in recent years include the magisterial *The Oxford History of the British Empire*, Wm. Roger Louis, ed. (Oxford: Oxford University Press, 1998–99). See especially volume III, *The Nineteenth Century*, Andrew Porter, ed. Trevor Lloyd's *Empire: The History of the British Empire* (London: Hambledon and London, 2001), is an excellent single volume account of the modern empire, as is that by Lawrence James, *The Rise and Fall of the British Empire* (New York: St. Martin's Press, 1996).

Finally, many of Gordon's more prominent contemporaries have been given close biographical treatment in which he figures. These include John

Pollock, *Kitchener: The Road to Omdurman* (London: Constable, 1998) Cromer comes under the scrutiny of Roger Owen in *Lord Cromer: Victorian Imperialist, Edwardian Proconsul* (Oxford: Oxford University Press, 2004). Viscount Wolseley is another important biographical subject for those interested in Britain's Victorian-era Imperial wars. See, for example, Joseph H. Lehmann, *All Sir Garnet: A Life of Field-Marshal Lord Wolseley* (London: Jonathan Cape, 1964). Also, Adrian Preston, ed., *In Relief of Gordon: Lord Wolseley's Campaign Journal of the Khartoum Relief Expedition, 1884-1885* (London: Hutchinson, 1967). Gordon's chief nemesis, the Mahdi, is given a contemporary examination by Fergus Nicoll, *The Mahdi of Sudan and the Death of General Gordon* (Stroud: Sutton, 2005).

About the Author

C. Brad Faught is Associate Professor of History and Chair of the Division of Arts at Tyndale University College in Toronto where he teaches in the areas of British and British Imperial history, as well as in that of Modern Europe and the First and Second World Wars. A graduate of the Universities of Oxford and Toronto, and a Fellow of the Royal Historical Society, he is the author of *The Oxford Movement: A Thematic History of the Tractarians and Their Times* (Pennsylvania State University Press, 2003).